# The Heart of the Father

Building Identity Through Intimacy

by

Jeremy Friedman

# The Heart of the Father

Building Identity Through Intimacy

by

Jeremy Friedman

Lighthouse Family Ministries, Inc.
www.LighthouseFM.net

The Heart of the Father:
*Building Identity Through Intimacy*

Requests for bulk sales discounts, editorial permissions, or other information should be addressed to:

Scroll Publishers
PO Box 5847
Pinehurst, NC 28374 USA

Additional copies available at www.ScrollPublishers.com

ISBN 13 TP: 978-1-962808-13-2
ISBN 13 eBook: 978-1-962808-14-9

Cover Design by Darian Horner Design
(www.darianhorner.com)
Image: elements.envato.com QKU4HLT

First Edition: January 2025

10 9 8 7 6 5 4 3 2 1 0

Printed in the United States of America

# Table of Contents

# Acknowledgements

This book is dedicated to the spiritual mentors who have poured into me and my family over the years, guiding us toward intimacy with the Lord as a foundational tenant of spiritual growth and development. I would like to thank my wife, Joelene, for her patience and support in our mission to build the family altar and for walking with me as we demonstrate seeking Him first before all else is paramount in all things.

Additionally, I would like to thank my spiritual family at LifeSpring International Ministries, Heart of Worship Church, and Habitation Church (formerly Safehouse) for the oil they have poured into our lives, provoking us to walk in sonship and deeper intimacy with God.

Finally, I wish to honor my longtime friend and mentor, Dr. Ron Horner, who has instructed me in the importance of journaling with Heaven and receiving revelation. Thank you for consistently pushing me out of my comfort zone to grow and expand spiritually.

# Foreword

This book is a must-read for anyone looking to move from merely reacting to life to living in victory. It's a transformative journey that opens the door to Kingdom adventures, inviting us to allow God to break down old patterns and replace them with Kingdom principles.

Jeremy shares with us the lessons he's learned over the past several years, revealing how Father has repositioned him and his family for much greater things than he ever imagined. While we all should cherish and trust God's Holy Word, we must also remember that there is a real-life component to the "living Word."

Through this book, Jeremy offers powerful personal insights into how Heaven operates and how we can access and benefit from it. One key takeaway is that we cannot fully carry God's presence if we hold on to old ways of thinking and living. These outdated patterns simply do not align with Kingdom principles.

Although not all of us may share Jeremy's gift of "seeing" into the spiritual realm, his detailed accounts provide us with a unique perspective on what's happening around us. Even if we perceive spiritual realities differently—through knowing, feeling, or hearing—we can still engage with and understand what is real in the spiritual realm.

As you read, take time to reflect on each experience and ask yourself, "How can this apply to me?"

Thank you, Jeremy, for being so transparent and allowing us to learn from your journey.

*– Dr. Robert Rodich*

# Recommendation for
# The Father's Heart

Jeremy is a deeply gifted and humble Seer Prophet of God. In this book, he shares extraordinary encounters with our Heavenly Father. As he is released to share these experiences, we can imagine the Father instructing him by His faithfulness and love.

For many within the Ecclesia Church, such encounters and visions might seem beyond comprehension. Why was Jeremy chosen for this? One verse comes to mind: *"Truly, I say to you, unless you turn and become like children, you will never enter the kingdom of heaven" (Matthew 18:3, ESV).*

Those who know Jeremy personally will recognize that this verse reflects his heart. His childlike faith and humility are why the Father can trust him with such incredible encounters.

I believe the purpose of these visions extends beyond Jeremy's personal journey. They are meant to help us grow in our faith and belief in a deeper understanding of God's

Kingdom. These encounters, shared publicly, serve to elevate and strengthen our collective faith.

If we can begin to grasp the depth of our Father's love in a way we have never experienced before, what could possibly stand in the way of the connection between Heaven and Earth? Could we dare to know the love of the Father in the same way that Enoch, Abraham, Moses, or David did? What did their hearts look like to God, and how were they shaped by His affection?

As you journey through this book, filled with valuable insights, I encourage you to ask the Father to increase your faith. My faith has grown immeasurably through Jeremy's testimony. I invite you to approach this journey with the same childlike belief that Jeremy demonstrates. Let us long for such rendezvous with the love of our Father!

The Kingdom of God is both expressive and sensitive, accessible only through the Spirit of God. If you are among those who have never known the love of an earthly father, it may be challenging to understand the deep, transformative love of our Heavenly Father. I urge you to ask the Holy Spirit to heal your heart and help you receive the boundless, unconditional love of your Creator.

This book will challenge you to submit to and humble yourself before a Father whose love is indescribable yet wholly attainable. It invites readers to explore the transformative power of God's love, a love that transcends human understanding but is available to all who seek it.

Jeremy, as the author of this incredible book, I know our Father is so pleased with you! He has entrusted you as one of his valuable, righteous scribes! Keep your ear to his heart for the Next! The Earth needs your faith and insight into our Father's great love for his creation! Until then, we are enlightened and transformed by the love you have so beautifully revealed in this book.

Eternally & affectionately,

*Karen Sumrall, "Nona"*

# Characters in this Book

Abraham: An Old Testament patriarch.

Charles Dickens: Author within the cloud of witnesses.

Daphne: An angel assigned to assist me in the realms of Heaven.

Dana: A man in white linen, part of my cloud of witnesses.

Daniel: An Old Testament prophet.

Danyal: Man in white, part of the cloud of witnesses.

Elijah: An Old Testament prophet.

Elisha: An Old Testament prophet.

Ernest Hemmingway: Author within the cloud of witnesses.

Ezekiel: An Old Testament prophet.

Gloria: A woman in white linen, part of my cloud of witnesses, who assists me with writing.

Isaac: An Old Testament patriarch.

Isaiah: An Old Testament prophet.

Jacob: An Old Testament patriarch.

Jeremiah: An Old Testament prophet.

Job: Old Testament patriarch.

Jonah: An Old Testament prophet.

John, the Beloved: The revelator and New Testament disciple.

Joseph: An Old Testament patriarch.

Joshua: An Old Testament prophet.

King David: An Old Testament monarch.

Lily: A personal angel, a commander under Phillip.

Lydia: A woman in the cloud of witnesses.

Mark Twain: Author within the cloud of witnesses.

Malachi: An Old Testament patriarch.

Manny: An angel who assists with writing.

Mitchell: A man in white who brings instruction from Heaven.

Moses: An Old Testament patriarch.

Noah: An Old Testament patriarch.

Peter: A New Testament apostle.

Phillip: My Chief personal angel.

Samuel: An Old Testament prophet.

# Preface

It is my greatest joy to share the material in this book with you and anyone the Father chooses to feed through the revelations, encounters, and experiences found within. This book is a collection of journal entries and revelatory encounters with the Father, born from a journey of learning to look to Him as the source of all things. Through this process, I have discovered that God alone is my validation, my worth, and my identity. It has led me to one undeniable conclusion: all people, at some point, will fail or disappoint us if we place our trust in them—but our Heavenly Father never will.

As you read, I invite you to step into each revelation and encounter. These pages are not merely words but an invitation from the Father to you. His messages have the power to transform you, deepen your intimacy with Him, and unlock His heart in ways you've never known.

As I completed the final touches on this book, I had an extraordinary experience. I was taken to a place in Heaven known as the Author's Symposium, located within Heaven's

Business Complex. This immense library was unlike anything I'd seen, and there I encountered three men: Mark Twain, Charles Dickens, and Ernest Hemingway.

My soul wrestled momentarily to comprehend what I was seeing. In disbelief, I muttered aloud, "Isn't Ernest Hemingway dead?" He chuckled and replied, "Dead as a doornail, but alive in Christ."

They led me down a grand corridor to a writer's desk equipped with what looked like a typewriter fused with the screen of a word processor. Near the desk was Gloria, an attendant in Heaven who assisted me with scrolls and manuscripts, and an angel named Manny.

As they greeted me and beckoned me to sit down, Manny said, "The time is near; the portals of the written Word have been opened. Seize this day and the opportunity to produce the works the Father wills for you to release in this hour. Only the sons will truly be able to access this place of intimacy and worship that the Father brings those He delights in to come and expand the knowledge and understanding He has in His vast library. Soak in the glory and knowledge and breathe in the revelation He is releasing. Write all that is in the scrolls before you, know as it is distributed upon the Earth, it will release the necessary revelation for others to be brought into the place of maturity and have their gift-mix finely tuned to truly represent the Father' heart in all things."

What you hold in your hands is a collection of love letters and revelations, a glimpse into the Father's thoughts and the posture of His heart toward His children. This book reflects the meditations of His heart, offering comfort and connection in times of need and longing for His presence. These words have been my source of strength during seasons of uncertainty, trials, and, most profoundly, the proving grounds of faith.

The Father desires fellowship with us. He longs for us to seek His presence, ask for His guidance, know Him deeply, and discover His heart. His invitation is for us to step into the Secret Place described in Matthew 6:6, where we can encounter Him intimately.

As you read this book, let the Father's words flow into your spirit and nourish you. Allow them to touch the wounded, broken, and weary places within your soul, guiding you toward your true identity as a *SON*. Here, "son" is a positional term reflecting our inheritance as adopted members of God's family. If you feel led, adapt the term to "daughter" or "child," but above all, let these words from the Father bring you solace in your current season.

May the words leap off the page and feed your spirit as you read them. May this book break off generational iniquities that have blinded and deafened the children of God from knowing Him and experiencing Him. The Word says that His sheep hear His voice, they recognize His voice, they heed to the sound of His voice.

> *Father, in Jesus' name, I pray for every person reading these words to be transformed by a deep revelation of their true worth in Yeshua (Jesus). May they come to know this truth at the very core of their being. Let every gap or weakness in their character be filled with the presence and power of the Holy Spirit, leaving no space for the adversary to exploit. I ask that You draw them closer to You—deeper into Your love—so they may fully embrace their true identity in Christ. Open the eyes of their hearts and understanding, allowing them to hear, see, and perceive You with fresh clarity and newness, beginning this very day, in Yeshua's name, Amen!*

My deepest hope is that, above all else, you will come away from these pages with a greater understanding of His unfailing love. The encounters shared here have profoundly impacted me—they have deepened my spiritual growth, shaped me into a better man, husband, and father, and guided me as a leader.

If you invite Jesus to be Lord over every part of your life and allow Him to take His rightful place on the throne of your heart, I am confident these truths will transform your life as they have mine. It is not just my hope but my firm belief that this book will lead you into deeper spiritual growth and a more intimate relationship with God. Enjoy the journey!

Love & Blessings,

*Jeremy*

# Chapter 1
## Searching to Know Him

One summer afternoon, as I lay on my bed with worship music playing softly in the background, I entered a time of soaking—quieting my heart and seeking the presence of God. I intentionally set aside my thoughts and cares, laying them at Jesus' feet and focused on Him. In that stillness, I began to hear the voice of the Father speaking to me.

He initiated a dialogue about our spiritual realms and their inner workings, saying,

*Much of the Church has been asleep at the wheel; My children perish for lack of knowledge.*

As His words settled in my heart, I began to grasp their weight. I came to understand that He was referring to the need for us to step into the place of transfiguration—transforming our mountains of influence, embracing our positions of authority, and claiming our inheritance. It is through this transformation that we gain access to the deep places of His heart, coming to know His mind and thoughts intimately.

The Father longs for friends who will fellowship with Him and share in His heart's desires. While the Church has long taught us about Jesus' love for us, we have not been taught how to truly love Him in return. The Father spoke to me, saying:

> *It is My desire for all My children to know Me deeply and intimately. It brings delight to My heart when I see them striving for the presence of Heaven. When distractions arise and try to pull them away, I am overjoyed when they press through those distractions to seek My peace and rest.*

Then, Heaven resounded with an echo that took my breath away: *"This knowledge will have a multiversal impact."*

As I reflected on what this meant, I began to realize that each of us is a realm within realms—a living structure that is a multiverse in itself. We are composed of worlds within worlds, universes within universes. Our minds house spirits within bodies intricately designed with organs, cells, circulatory systems, nervous systems, neural pathways, neurons, and even microscopic ecosystems, all working together in astounding harmony.

The magnitude of this revelation stirred something deep within me. It was as though my soul struggled to comprehend such infinite complexity. A tension built within my chest, and I instinctively addressed it. I declared aloud, "Soul, step back, be at rest and peace. Body be at rest and peace. Spirit, come forward and bring ease to my soul in Jesus' name." As I began to pray in tongues, I could feel things shift. My soul grew quiet, the tension dissolved, and a profound sense of alignment took its place.

In that moment of stillness, a deeper truth began to emerge. The Father wasn't just speaking about the intricacy of creation; He was revealing His heart. Every part of our being—spiritual, mental, and physical—was crafted to reflect His glory and to engage in relationship with Him. The multiverse within us, though vast and complex, exists not for its own sake but to house His presence and to manifest His Kingdom.

In that moment, I understood that the complexity of all creation is so intricate and beyond all comprehension. I saw how often I had lived tethered to earthly patterns of thought—bound by fear, doubt, and self-imposed limitations. But here was the Creator of all things, inviting me into a boundless reality where His love transforms, heals, and restores every part of who I am. The Father is looking for sons and friends He can share with. I heard the Holy Spirit whisper to my heart:

*Be as one ready to receive with an open heart,
and more revelation will come. The Father desires
to have you know His heart, His thoughts, His
dreams and His deepest desires. Will you allow His
love to fill you and bring you past your limits?*

I prayed and said, "Father, I want to know You more, I want to know Your heart, I want You to fill me and help me grow beyond my limits; Lord, remove from me the earthly confines that are no heavenly good, ruin me and break me so you can heal me and fill me. Help me know Your radiant, fiery, hot love, that I will never be the same, forever changed and completely undone, when your presence comes. In Jesus name Amen!"

## Cease from Striving

In another instance, as I wrestled with surrendering circumstances beyond my control to the Father, the Holy Spirit spoke these words to give me perspective and understanding. He said:

*Be still, child. There is much in which you strive
to control; all things will play out at their appointed
times. Do not fret or fear but know that even the
circumstances that you're living through that are
most intolerable are used for your growth and the
growth of those around you and those you love so*

4

*dearly.[1] Without the test, there would be no testimony; without the trials, it would be hard to bear good fruit. Persevere through all things knowing that My love for you is so deep, so everlasting, but there is nothing that can tear that away from you and nothing that can tear you away from Me.*

*Be still and seek Me with your whole heart, coming to My presence when you need to be refreshed or refilled and know that I walk with you side-by-side. I am here to carry you when you're weak. The mysteries of heavenly realities will unfold to you in time as they are appointed to be released, but for now, seek first the Kingdom of God, and all things will be added onto you.[2] My child, you are stamped with the stamp of righteousness; the emblem of the Kingdom of God is the radiance seen on your countenance, the name on your forehead known only by the Lord God. You are one with Him and united with Him in spirit and in truth. The true path to peace and joy is only found in Him. When you search deep*

---

[1] "Now we know that all things work together for good for those who love God, who are called according to His purpose." (Romans 8:28 TLV)

[2] "But seek first the Kingdom of God and His righteousness, and all these things shall be added to you." (Matthew 6:33 TLV)

*within, you can find the presence of God deep within the Secret Place; this is your shared space to spend time with the Father and rejoice in His presence.*

The time spent entwined with the Father will help mold your heart, and you will, in turn, reflect His nature, His character, and His glory—just as Moses' face glistened when he came down from Mount Sinai, so you will glow with the radiance of the Father. Allow yourself time to be enraptured and enjoy the intimate moments; intimacy with the Father creates transformation. Transformation creates Christlikeness. Christ is in you, My dear child. Seek first the Kingdom of God and His righteousness; seek first the king of kings and the Lord of lords; this is what you were created for, to dwell and bask in His majesty.

## Encounter with the Father

In a profound encounter, I was taken into the Throne Room of Heaven. As I stood before the Throne of God, Jesus approached me and, with a gentle yet powerful motion, reached inside me, pulling my spirit out of my body. In a single motion, He flung it high into the air like a ball. To my astonishment, my spirit hit the surface of a vast ocean. As I made contact, my spirit began swimming in the cool waters.

Rising to the surface, I realized I was far from what seemed to be the shoreline. This experience defied earthly logic, but I came to understand that the ways of Heaven far surpass our understanding. As I swam towards the shore, I marveled at the deep, radiant blue of the water, unlike anything I had seen on Earth. The brilliance of its hue was mesmerizing. As I neared the shore, I noticed the sand—a stunning, sparkling white gold—glistening in the sunlight. I was soon crawling up the shore, feeling the sand cover me, its texture soft yet firm.

I noticed a tortoise before me and a sandpiper on the beach to my right, scurrying around. I saw Jesus just sitting there, gazing at me with a big, glorious smile. There were angels and saints beside Him, and as He watched me exploring this eternal paradise, I could feel the glory of His presence on my back and shoulders. It was warm, pure and holy. It comforted me like the sun beating down on me on a warm summer day.

I saw a coconut lying in the sand, which I picked up and smashed against a nearby rock. To my amazement, inside the coconut were gemstones and diamonds. Feeling led by the Spirit, I ate them, and as I did, I experienced their sweetness, like honey. These gemstones were not merely precious stones; they were revelations of the Father's goodness. As I consumed them, I tasted and saw how good He truly is.

As I stood up to walk, I stumbled into a sand trap, which opened up into a swirling slide that deposited me on a throne. This throne was adorned with red cushions and gold trim on the arms. Looking around, I realized that I had returned to the place where the encounter began. The room was immense, and I saw steps leading up to a platform where the throne rested.

I realized I was seated at the right hand of the Father.[3] I saw Him on a platform, slightly elevated from where I was, seated on His throne. He was looking at me, but from the shimmering, radiant intensity of the light coming from His face, I could not make out His figure. But I could sense His presence—His warmth, His smile, full of love, compassion, hope, and everything good I could ever experience. It was an overwhelming emotion of pure, unfailing love, washing over me.

As I breathed in this love, basking in its warm glow, I felt His hand gently caress my cheek. In a soft, loving whisper, He said, *"You are My beloved son, you are My most cherished, you are My most prized, with you I am so pleased."* I replied, "Wrap me in your arms, Papa." He picked

---

[3] "If then you were raised with Christ, seek those things which are above, where Christ is, sitting at the right hand of God." (Colossians 3:1)

me up and cradled me in His arms like a newborn baby, and I felt smothered in the bliss and ecstasy of His love.

## Another Heavenly Encounter:
## A Season of Transformation

In another remarkable encounter, I found myself in a vast courtyard, surrounded by many men and women dressed in white linen. They stood in awe, worshipping the Father in reverence. Suddenly, the Lord appeared before me as the Lion of Judah. I climbed onto His back, holding onto His mane, and we began to ride together. As He moved, He transformed into a man, and before us stood the throne of God.

Before the throne were the four living creatures described in Revelation 4, leading the worship, and around us, angels and saints joined in adoration. The Lord spoke to me, expressing His pride in how I had persevered through the trials and tests of the season. As I took in the scene, I noticed angels being instructed to remove my current garments and replace them with new ones. These new garments resembled white generals' uniforms, signifying authority and honor. Jesus smiled at me and pinned a gold star to my lapel, as a soldier would be decorated for valor.

My personal angels, Philip and Lily, were also being given new gear and receiving an increase in rank, stature and appearance. They stood at attention and received orders in which they were given charge over other commanders and ranks of angels that would co-labor with them for new assignments from Heaven. I saw next to Jesus many of the saints of old, all wearing white linen. Moses, Peter, Elijah, Elisha, Isaiah, and Joshua were all in attendance, standing by and watching.

The Father walked over, marveling at this gathering. He spoke of His deep love for me and how proud He was of my overcoming the adversity I had faced. This had been a season of crushing, and as I wept at this outpouring of His love, I pulled my heart out of my chest, held it in my hands before Him, and asked Him to heal its broken places. He poured the blood of Jesus over my heart and upon my hands. Immediately, my heart, my hands, and my whole body turned pure white as snow. As this new wholeness had come upon me, this engagement ended, but the mark He left upon me did not. This began the yearning and hunger for more profound, intimate encounters with Him.

# Chapter 2

# The Court of Destiny

As I grew in the revelation of intimacy with the Father and His unfailing love, I felt a strong urgency to dedicate a specific time each morning to seek Him. During one such moment of communion, I entered a vision where the Lord handed me three keys. Understanding that keys are used to unlock things in the natural world, I inquired about their purpose. The Holy Spirit prompted me to examine the vision more closely, and I became aware that we were inside a room filled with drawers, each with its own keyhole.

When I attempted to pull the handles, I quickly realized the drawers were locked. Heaven revealed that this place was known as the Court of Destiny within the Father's Kingdom. As I explored the space to understand it better, I noticed that it resembled a grand study or library. My attention was drawn to a specific area within this vast place, and I received instructions to use the keys to open two particular drawers.

I proceeded to unlock and open the first drawer, carefully pulling out its contents. Inside, I found a book, which was part of a larger collection. As I held it, the Holy Spirit began to explain the purpose of each book, unveiling deeper layers of understanding about the Father's plans and purposes.

The first book I retrieved was a book of destiny, specifically detailing the plans and purposes for leaders within the church I was serving at the time of this encounter. At that point in my life, I was actively involved as a board member and participating in several ministries. However, this season marked a profound shift in my spiritual journey. The Lord was gently but unmistakably drawing me away from religion and into a deeper, more intimate relationship with Him.

This shift awakened an insatiable hunger for God's presence and the deeper truths of His kingdom. My heart was changing rapidly. As I continued to draw closer to Him, I found it hard to serve in the capacity I had been called to. Things within my heart were rapidly changing; I was becoming increasingly grieved at the way God would show up in service, and just as His sweet presence came, we humans would push His presence aside to move to the next thing. We had adapted to a culture of drive-through churchianity and had gotten away from the altar and intimacy with the Lord. I started noticing the place I was in resembled the world and was not operating in the power of the Holy Spirit I was reading about in the Bible.

At the time of this encounter, I was seeking the Lord's perfect will for where I was to be rooted. Things seemed to be misaligned in my life, my family, and spiritually. What made things even more intense was that I had begun to hear God for myself. Weeks earlier, the Holy Spirit had spoken to me during a church service and said, *"Do you know you are in the wrong house?"* In the following weeks, I tried to remain accountable for what I had committed to as a man, but my spirit desired to follow the Lord. I was at a crossroads of serving man and knowing I needed to break free from religion and choose to serve God. Not only did I know it, but so did the Father, and He wanted me to break free from fear of man and serve Him.

Together, we opened the book for this place; as we turned the pages, I could see there were listings of leaders, board members, and pastors for various points of time. As we turned from the year 2020 to the year 2021, I didn't see my name written any longer on its pages. I was puzzled by this; however, the Father started to inform me and confirm what I was sensing in the spirit. Heaven showed me that there was a misalignment in my walk at this time.

He and I began to walk down the hallway towards the second drawer. As I unlocked and opened this drawer, inside was a book called, *The Book of Life and Destiny*. We opened it together and started to look at what was written inside. We could see the chronicles of various instances of time and happenings from my youth. We turned the pages forward to the year 2021, and the Father appeared, showing me a page indicating this was a time of rebirth, sanctification, and new beginnings for our family.

The Father told me this is the beginning of new things that will not look like the former things, that all go through stages of growth. Father said,

> *It is in the uncomfortable places that we experience the greatest growth. Be still, child. Allow the process to take its course; worry for nothing because all your days are in My hands; aim to do My will, and all will be well. Your heart already has the things I have put in it. Walk in My ways and seek My peace.*

His encouragement continued:

> *Don't look at your circumstances as a negative. This is a time of rebuilding; to build a new thing, sometimes buildings need to be razed to the ground, and out of the rubble will rise the new; the gestation period is over, and now is a period of rebirth. Let nothing distract you, but keep your eyes and ears focused on Heaven; all will be well. Leave your troubles at the cross and your burdens at My feet; I will carry you when you are weak; I will uphold you to be strong. My love for you is endless. Trust in Me.*

# The Warrior's Heart

One April morning in 2021, as I sat with the Father seeking His wisdom for the day, I heard Heaven say:

> *You are in the roaring twenties when many will hear the roar of the Lion of Judah. Many will come to faith and return to their first love in this time. Likewise, many will go in the opposite direction, and the roar will be against those who prefer the paths of wickedness. Choose wisely, My son; do not follow the path of death; the broad way leads to destruction. Happy are the ones who overcome the testing and endure till the end for My name's sake.*

In a subsequent encounter the following day, I was pressing in for more revelation on what was formerly shared. I was brought into Heaven and found myself riding on a train that arrived out front of Father's house. As I arrived, Yeshua asked me, "What do you see?" I took a breath, focused intently, and looked onward, straining to see. I knew He was training me to operate more effectively in the seer anointing. I noticed a flock of ducks and swans swimming in a lake with their young. Heaven said, *"It is a new season, one of rebirth and revival."*

The scripture Isaiah 60 came to mind, and I heard its words in the spirit:

*Arise, shine, for your light has come! The glory of ADONAI has risen on you. For behold, darkness covers the Earth, and deep darkness the peoples. But ADONAI will arise upon you, and His glory will appear over you. Nations will come to your light, kings to the brilliance of your rising. Lift up your eyes and look all around: they all gather—they come to you—your sons will come from far away, your daughters carried on the hip. Then you will see and be radiant, and your heart will throb and swell with joy. For the abundance of the sea will be turned over to you. The wealth of nations will come to you. A multitude of camels will cover you, young camels of Midian and Ephah, all those from Sheba will come. They will bring gold and frankincense and proclaim the praises of ADONAI. All Kedar's flocks will be gathered to you. Nebaioth's rams will minister to you. They will go up with favor on My altar, and I will beautify My glorious House.*

*Who are these who fly like a cloud, like doves to their windows? Surely the islands will hope in Me, with the ships of Tarshish in the lead, to bring your sons from afar, their silver and gold with them, for the Name of ADONAI your God, and for the Holy One of Israel, because He has glorified you. Foreigners will build up your walls, and their kings will minister to you. For in My fury, I struck you, but in My favor, I will show you mercy. Your gates will be open continually. They will not be shut day or night so that men may bring to you the wealth of the nations, with their kings led in procession. (Isaiah 60:1-11, TLV)*

As I focused back on the vision, I could see two wild horses like bucking broncos barreling toward us, and I heard the Holy Spirit say, *"With the word of authority, you will tame the bucking broncos."*

I spoke the word 'peace' with my hands raised, and instantly, they both settled and came to a complete halt before us. The Holy Spirit gave me specific instructions; He said:

*Speak peace into all situations that seem to be lacking in it; the audible release of the Word of the Lord will transform those atmospheres like Jesus in the storm with the disciples. You will see the storms still.*

Holy Spirit then encouraged me:

*You are a warrior; you have been given a warrior's heart. Don't allow your surroundings to make you battle-weary. Retreat to rest in My glorious presence. The love of the Father is more than enough to soothe all that is bothering you. The world and its works will only sting and hinder that which the Father wants to heal.*

*The world is like salt in a wound; it will sting where the Father's love will smooth and comfort. Pause to rest in His presence. Greater is He that is in you. Stand firm in the Father's faith, let that be your faith, let your spirit rise and pour out the fire of fervent prayer that all plants He hath not planted will be licked up with the flame. I will never fail to forsake you, My beloved; you are My everything, you are My true love, and I am madly in love with you; you are My favorite creation; there is none more unique and special than you, My dear one. Always remember you are My beloved!*

In another engagement, I was wrestling with feelings of being broken down and beaten. I proceeded to seek the presence of the Lord as I needed encouragement. I was learning to come out of the orphan mindset religion had instilled in me and not judge myself harshly for just being human. As I allowed the Father to cultivate the identity of sonship with me, I still wrestled with feelings of inadequacy. The comfort of the Father was much needed to reassure me of who I was from His perspective. As He spoke into my heart, I could see I had been taking the bait of the enemy.

The Father said,

*My son, you are so beloved; you can make mistakes. This is how you learn, but leave no room for the enemy and his lies to worm his way in and deceive your heart. His words are as rotten fruit, and when they plant a root, it will bear bad fruit. But the word of life bears roots downward and brings good fruit upward that will build you up and be nourishment to build up nations.*

He informed me that He was also instilling a precious gift upon me during this hour as this process was being worked out. He said, *"I am giving you the key to the nations."* As He said this, I saw myself praying for people from other tribes. He continued:

*Stay in the cleft of the rock, like a baby in its mother's bosom. When you hide yourself in Shaddai, nothing can shake your foundation. Jesus came to set the captives free, but I have given you the keys to unlock the shackles of those that are bound.*

## Heaven's Validation

In another encounter, which occurred on my daily commute to work, I was taken into an open vision. In the spirit, I could see we entered a place of prayer and intercession for the Lord's blessings, which was called the Court of Favor. As I entered the golden glow of this place, sitting in front of me was new armor and a treasure chest. I was given two keys and immediately, like a child on Christmas morning, dove towards the chest to open it. As I put the key inside the lock and turned it to open it, to my surprise, the chest was filled with popcorn, oil, and butter. Immediately, a verse from Job dropped into my spirit:

*When my steps were washed with butter, and the rock poured out for me streams of oil. (Job 29:6, KJV)*

I heard the Holy Spirit say that my steps are bathed in favor, in oil and butter; I reached into the chest and spread it all over myself. As I engaged in this prophetic action, I could feel the anointing pouring out.

I then noticed a silver door and quickly used the other key to unlock it. As the door opened, I was greeted by the spirits of Knowledge, Wisdom, and Revelation. I was informed that I had entered a realm I understood to be the Court of Men & Women in White. I saw many saints around, but my eyes widened as I noticed Abraham, Isaac, and Jacob. They approached me and began to trade into my life by speaking their faith into me. As they spoke, they laid hands upon me, and there was a transference of anointing and gifts that were imparted to expand my faith in God. I was told that this was the Father's faith.

In another spiritual engagement, I requested access to the Help Desk of Heaven and was greeted by a man named Danyal. He asked what I needed, and I shared my desire for a mentor who could guide me in understanding and operating in the prophetic.

I was then escorted to a classroom and greeted by two other figures, Mitchell and Lydia. As I took a seat behind a desk, they began to instruct me, using a chalkboard to illustrate their teachings. They started to instruct me about the prophetic and my desire in this season to truly understand the call of God upon my own life in a greater depth. They began to instruct me on the weight and responsibility of those with prophetic mantles and the office of the prophet. Lydia explained the different gifts, signs, wonders, and miracles that prophets walk in. Mitchell explained to me how some have balanced gifts across many avenues, while others are more proficient in a few gifts and not always as proficient in others. They explained how this related to me, where I was called to, and that I was growing into these things in both natural & supernatural realms.

This was a time of great perplexity at my job and the church I was in at this time of my life. The pain of growth at times had me wanting to call it quits, but Heaven said:

> *You are learning practical applications for ministry, so don't cut short the harvest time. Be still and know I am God. The conflict you feel is the fight between the Earth-ruled realm and your spirit's desire to be free to do the work of the Kingdom of God. The season is coming for the advancement (you seek), but for now, walk in this way as you are being prepared for what is yet to*

*come. You are beloved; you are precious, and you are making a difference.*

Suddenly, I went into an open vision; I saw a campfire and one standing before it. The fire spread from the one before it to all the others encircled around the fire. One by one, they were set ablaze; it was like a domino effect of the fire, and hunger for God was spreading rapidly around this circle. Holy Spirit spoke and said the circle represented a community of believers. Insinuating that as the fire stirred within me, I could spread it to others, and my hunger for God would stir the hunger in others.

Holy Spirit said:

*Be still, child, and know you serve Me independently of earthly confines. Your allegiance to the Kingdom of Heaven has not gone unnoticed, and your demeanor is commendable. Continue to seek the Kingdom and the Lord's righteousness first, and all that you seek to do shall flourish like a cedar in Lebanon that the rivers of the Lord have watered. Let love radiate from your heart into all the outer reaches of your territories, for this love is the Father's love, and it is the light that shines from hilltops, lighting the path for those lost in the dark. Carry on, good and faithful servant, carry on!*

As I listened, I became aware of my personal angel Phillip's presence. He said:

*Stop seeking (meaning other jobs). You are searching out of your soul realm; there is an assignment that has been given to you until the time of completion has arrived, and the next assignment is on the horizon. The Father is doing a new thing in your life. Don't let the frequencies around you distract your mind from the Father's work. Glorify His name by being a good steward.*

*By cheerfully and gladly doing the tasks you dislike, or feel are demeaning and meaningless, you are humbling yourself to do good work in His name. This can be viewed as akin to the son of God, Jesus the Messiah, washing the feet of his students. As you submit to that which the Father is giving into your hand to plow and harvest, you will feel an ease and a rest that you have not yet felt as your soul has been fighting against this.*

*Your mind has been running rampant and working overtime. Sit, breathe, and be still in the Father's presence; all His promises for you will come to pass. He does not require your help to establish them; just be obedient to the Spirit of the Living God, and the commissioning His Spirit speaks to you as His son, his general, and His minister in this mission field.*

# Chapter 3

# Walk in Love

The ministry of the Holy Spirit in the lives of God's children is both profound and transformative. One morning, during my time in the Secret Place with the Father, my devotional led me to 1 John 4.

As I read, the words seemed to leap off the page, and I found myself drawn into a divine encounter with the Holy Spirit.

In this sacred moment, He began to speak to me about the importance of solidifying our identity in Christ. He revealed that this process is foundational to walking fully in the Father's love. The Holy Spirit then guided me to Isaiah and impressed upon me the importance of meditating deeply on these words:

*¹ Arise, shine; For your light has come! And the glory of the Lord is risen upon you. ² For behold, the darkness shall cover the Earth, and deep darkness the people; but the Lord will arise over you, and His glory will be seen upon you. ³ The Gentiles shall come to your light and kings to the brightness of your rising. ⁴ Lift up your eyes all around, and see: they all gather together, they come to you; your sons shall come from afar, and your daughters shall be nursed at your side. ⁵ Then you shall see and become radiant, and your heart shall swell with joy; because the abundance of the sea shall be turned to you, the wealth of the Gentiles shall come to you. (Isaiah 60:1-5)*

As I sat and pondered the words I had just read, the Holy Spirit spoke and said:

*My love shall saturate and overwhelm you. It will soak you down to every cell in your being and flow forward into the lives of those around you. Live yielded to the rivers of the love of the Father. Live in this place of overwhelming ecstasy and union with the Father. Enter rest and worship. It is the best warfare against earthen frequencies. Focus on Heaven and allow yourself to be transformed in His Glory.*

His instruction continued, and He informed me that my heart posture needed some correction. In this season, I was learning to *love beyond my own limits*. I would often get offended at those who would persecute me with words or those with religious mindsets that I was not seeing eye to eye with. The Father's voice broke in, admonished me, and said:

*Be kind to all those you meet because their time will come, and all are mine. Even those of your own house who are not yet postured towards Me. There will be a day when all will be on My threshing floor. Be as wheat, flexible against the wind, going to and fro, steadfast in readiness and preparation for the day when the wheat will be made into bread. Does the wheat complain at its time of preparation and wait for harvest? Does it scream or groan as it is hard-pressed to be used for that which provides nourishment?*

"No," I responded, although I knew His question was rhetorical. Holy Spirit continued:

*Be still and know you are blessed among people and loved by the Father more than your soul or mind can comprehend. The Father's love for you and His beloved children runs deeper than the depths of the sea. His love is like an overwhelming torrent. Let it wash over you and release all your burdens to Him. Lighten your load and allow yourself to experience the true rest that comes from being still in the presence of the Lord.*

In a subsequent engagement, I was taken into a vision and was looking at a vast crystal ocean with a rainbow above it and a bright light on the horizon. The scene shifted to one where I was worshipping on my knees before the Throne of God. I knelt, and as I did, I kissed Jesus' feet and saw the nail marks. As I looked around, I noticed three angels were standing before me holding staffs, and one spoke to me, saying, "Rise up." Another handed me a mace and said this was for tearing down strongholds.

Then, the Lord picked me up and carried me like a small child laid in His arms; then I saw the mace get swung at a brick wall, and the wall exploded, bricks flew everywhere, and I heard the words, *"Walls are falling down."* As I continued to engage with Heaven, I saw myself dressed in armor at the foot of a mountain, fighting against a large, formidable foe. As I fought valiantly, I lunged forward and plunged a sword into the belly of this beast. As the beast was slain, it disappeared, and in its place, a keyhole remained with light shining through it.

I heard that on the other side of this mountain, there is a great blessing. I had a knowing in my spirit that this mountain represented pain relating to some things my spouse was experiencing at this time. As a family, we were in a time of transition, leaving a place we had served in yet had been hurt by a spirit of religion. Yet in faithfulness, Father had prepared another place and was in the process of leading us to it.

In the spirit, I saw the nation of Israel and heard the Holy Spirit say the words, *"Land of milk and honey."*

I got the impression that this burden was merely a trial that an individual must overcome in faith and to press through. Though it felt like warfare, it was simply the Father's love presenting a time of testing and refining to possess the good things he wanted to bestow on us. As I sought His Word for confirmation, he led me to these scriptures:

> *³ The floods have lifted up, O LORD, the floods have lifted up their voice; the floods lift up their waves. ⁴ The LORD on high is mightier than the noise of many waters, than the mighty waves of the sea. (Psalms 93:3-4)*

> *So shall they fear the name of the LORD from the west, And His glory from the rising of the sun; When the enemy comes in like a flood, the Spirit of the LORD will lift up a standard against him. (Isaiah 59:19)*

## Walking Through the Second Heaven

On another adventure-filled day with Papa (Father God), I stepped into Heaven. I immediately saw myself walking with my angels across a rainbow path that arched from the Earth to the second heaven. I could see many dark entities and it was explained to me that these were the forces that blocked prayer and subdued the faith of people. I could see many whose lives were impacted by allowing these dark things access to their homes, minds and lives through the ungodly things they gave attention to in the Earth realm.

As we continued walking through this area, I could see a golden door; this door led to the Throne Room of God. We entered, and I saw Father. I ran up, bowed low, and gave Him a big hug. I then saw, before the throne, a book with a blank page. The Father explained this was the choice of free will. Father explained it is the part of human life where we are given the capacity to choose to live by God's will or our own will. I declared that I chose God's will, and instantly, the page was filled with writing, this was the writing of my destiny according to the will of the Father.

He asked if I was ready, and His palm hit my chest. My body bowed low to the ground, but my spirit flew out from above. As I surveyed the ground below, I could see many surrounding me In Heaven. I could see the living creatures, angels, and saints around the throne. John, the beloved, Yeshua's disciple, spoke to me and laid his hands up on me.

As he spoke, he informed me this was Heaven's way of trading through prayer impartation. He then imparted the depth of the Father's love for me. I could feel the power of this impartation overwhelming me to an emotional point; I wept and then was shown in a vision how my life in the past had been impacted by self-will. My past was shown to me, and I could see, prior to my salvation, how I had been influenced by worldly living and had allowed dark things to dominate my life and choices. I was shown past instances when the Lord was calling to me, but I was more focused on worldly pleasures.

The scene changed, and He showed me Heaven's standpoint of the night He intervened to get me back on track, how He saved me and called me to Himself. As the encounter concluded, He gave me scriptures to meditate on, confirming His purpose for my life. We are all predestined for greatness and predestined to experience his great love.

*Before I formed you in the womb I knew you; Before you were born, I sanctified you; I ordained you as a prophet to the nations. (Jeremiah 1:5)*

*Such knowledge is too wonderful for me; it is high, I cannot attain it. (Psalms 139:6)*

# Chapter 4

# His Love Brings Forth Deliverance

The following encounters occurred during instances of prayer in which I was engaged in generational cleansing from the sins of my ancestors and their engagements in secret societies and Freemasonry. For those who may have an interest in purging these sins from their bloodlines, I recommend the book *Overcoming the False Verdicts of Freemasonry* by Dr. Ron M. Horner.[4] The following journal details and encounters I had that were so amazing I could not resist including them to display our Father's heart.

One afternoon, as I was praying in the Courts of Heaven regarding my family's involvement in Freemasonry, the Father took me into a vision and revelatory encounter. I had been repenting for myself, my wife, and our bloodlines past, present, and future. As I prayed, I saw the spirits of all these

---

[4] Ron M. Horner, *Overcoming the False Verdicts of Freemasonry* (LifeSpring Publishing, 2018), https://ronhorner.com.

generations gathered in the courtroom before Jesus. Many were weeping and expressing sorrow and grief for the iniquities of the past that impacted future generations. As the case was settled and judged by the Just Judge, Jesus Himself invited us to take communion.

Suddenly, the scene changed from the courtroom to all these individuals outside, by a lake in Heaven. There was lush green grass all around; the scene was beautiful. Jesus led us in communion, and then a portal opened that allowed all the other souls to step through. Jesus walked over to me, and we started talking. He opened another portal to take me into "my Secret Place."

At this moment, a dream I had the night before involving a scroll and angels was clarified to me as a message of protection for myself and my family. Jesus then told me that someone wished to meet with me. As another gate opened, I saw King David step through and approach me.

He began to speak to me about ministering from a place of rest and how vitally important this was to everything I was to do for different ministries, my family, and my job. King David explained how to pray into this and walk into this rest while engaging Heaven at the same time. Heaven knew my life and times and could see in the natural as I lived in these moments but was easily frustrated. King David explained how important love was in these equations. When he finished talking, the three of us stepped through another gate, where we were in the throne room before the Father.

The Father had a book in hand. It was the book of my life and destiny. He flipped it open, and to my surprise, we were looking at what was written about the 70th year of my life. Decade by decade, he went backward in time, in 10-year intervals, highlighting a specific miracle I was to bear witness to in those years. 70 was the dissipation of a cancerous tumor, 50 or 60 was the raising of the dead, 40 was a greater impartation of the prophetic gifts and seeing in the spirit, should I follow his path for my life.

I was advised that when I perceive the presence of angels, I seek from the Holy Spirit how to partner with them to do the Father's will. I don't recall all he had shown because it was so much. It was so profound and explosive that I was overwhelmed by his love and felt as if I was drinking from a fire hose of living water. The Father explained that at this time, I was in my "teething years," and my feelings of inadequacy were just feelings of growing and maturing at the rate I was to grow into sonship.

He revealed much of my children's lives. Alexander and Genevieve would have a double portion of this mantle on their lives. He showed that Brianna, Jack, and Gianluca would have some of their struggles in life that would turn out to be testimonies, and all of them would willfully choose Jesus. Jack was the one who seemed to hold truest to the teaching of the Bible and prayer of the three as a means to get through these times, as shown to me. He handed me a box, and inside it was a ruby heart that radiated a red light of intention and love. Its radiance penetrated my life, my body, soul, and family. It was a gift of his love for my marriage and family for us to steward His love. He explained that I must foster love into the lives of my wife and children. I was told to give more love to them, as much of the battles on the home front during this year, 2020, were just cries for attention and more love or individual attention.

Father acknowledged the deep things of my heart regarding the houses of worship I served in that season. He explained I was at both for a reason during that time. He showed me the bond registries for myself and my family and revealed that the Father still hears the prayers of those who are stuck in religion and registers them as blessings on our behalf. Although they do not yet know His son, He hears and loves them. Some of the bonds that were logged for me were the prayers of my earthly Father. The Lord showed me they are drawing closer to the time of his choosing for them to know Him but emphasized it was not for me to know. I was told to inspect the registries, at which point the spirit led me to severing ungodly bonds and issuing godly ones over the ministries, the congregations, the ministry teams, and those in positions of authority.

The Father applauded me and told me how proud He was that I was doing this. He wanted to demonstrate how He sees the importance of my walk and that I shouldn't be held up in the politics of boards, ministries, and the opinions of the flesh but rather to walk and radiate his love in all things. He always demonstrated to me the keen ability of knowing with my knower as a means of seeing in the spirit.

Then, the Father refocused back on me, and He acknowledged that He heard the cries of my heart. He knew I longed to walk with Him, as other generals of the faith had done, such as Smith Wigglesworth and John G. Lake.

He knew my longing and desire to see the types of miracles that bring Glory to God. Father extended his arm towards me and forcefully struck my heart with a firm open-hand strike; as He did this, my spirit flew backward out of my body and then came back into my body. When my spirit re-joined my body, my whole being vibrated with what I assumed to be the frequency of Heaven. I could feel a heavy anointing, and He explained to me how He had basically unlocked this gifting that would begin to flourish in me at new levels. I was so moved that I physically fell to my knees, tears flowing from my eyes, and worshipped. I was utterly overcome and undone by his goodness and by just how much He knows the deepest desires of our hearts.

# Baptism By Fire

As I continued to engage with Heaven, I had a separate encounter in which I experienced a Baptism of Fire. This fire was representative of the Father's fiery love that changes and transforms.

In this engagement, I noticed I was standing on a balcony with the Father, viewing the whole Earth. I saw lightning strikes and a sea of angels. Father showed me how people were unblinded and freed from these prayers of repentance. I was told their eyes would be able to see the light of the world, Jesus. He handed me a key, and next to Him was a chest that would unlock. As I dug into the chest, I found a scroll that read like a love letter of adoration commending and encouraging me inside. As I continued to pull things out of this chest, I found a shield for my heart to guard it from darkness and the lies of the world. Father said:

> *Save the key until a later time when I will reveal how you are to use it. It is the season of return, child, returning to Me, not to a church, not to a house of prayer, a returning to My courts. I am assembling an army of the nations. This is a time of rising up, resurrection, and equipping against those operating in rebellion. Hold fast to what you have been given and to what you have learned. Prepare your heart; now is the season when all is being made new by My presence. New wineskins*

*are being filled. New scrolls are being released, and*
*new mandates are being fulfilled; return with all*
*your heart, soul, mind, and strength, and I will*
*sustain and carry you to greater realms of Glory. I*
*am stripping away all religious ties that bind.*

As the Father spoke this to me, I saw in the spirit what appeared as a jar of dice being shaken. He whispered, *"I am shaking things up."*

Looking again into the vision, I saw myself on a tire tube, going through choppy waters like a raft going over white-water rapids. I saw that Jesus was with me, suddenly the waters became still, and He said, *"I am the raft that sustains you and holds you."*

As we moved on from this place, Jesus walked ahead, his head wrapped in his shawl; He was carrying a shepherd's crook. He turned and anointed my head with oil, and as He did, I could feel the presence of the Holy Spirit flowing over me. He said to me, *"You are a Glory Carrier."*

In another instance, I was taken into a vision in which I saw water droplets falling; as my gaze focused on the scene ahead, I noticed I was standing near a river, which was flowing calmly. Jesus said that this was the River of Peace.

As I walked along the riverbanks, we saw children playing and animals nearby. We came to a cave with big, locked doors. The Lord handed me a key and told me it was the Cave of Wonders. We unlocked the doors, and as we entered in, I noticed this was a place where signs, wonders, and miracles were held. This was a place where I could view things from an eternal perspective and witness many events. Some of the events I viewed had transpired in the past, while others had not yet come to pass. This place exemplified the power of the Lord God through his wonders. As I beheld the beauty of this place, the Lord said to me:

> *I am setting you up to minister in places you would not ordinarily go to pray. My Glory will flow through you. Do not fear the world or what dwells there but be obedient to go to My children.*

As this engagement ended, He left me with the following scripture from Isaiah to feed my spirit man and process what had been shared:

> *Comfort, comfort My people,' says your God. Speak kindly to the heart of Jerusalem and proclaim to her that her warfare has ended, that her iniquity has been removed. For she has received from ADONAI's hand double for all her sins. A voice cries out in the wilderness, 'Prepare the way of ADONAI; make straight in the desert a highway for our God. (Isaiah 40:1-3, TLV)*

As you continue to seek the Father, allow his fire to cleanse and purify you. Allow it to transform your heart. The baptism of fire comes by invitation and seeking the deeper things of God. Invite His fire to come into your life and lean into the process by which He will take you from Glory to Glory.

# Chapter 5
# Half Dead Inside

While traveling to work the morning of May 8th, 2021, I was taken into a revelatory encounter. As I was brought into Heaven to receive revelation, I found myself dwelling in a place called the Court of Favor. In this vision, I was greeted by Peter the Apostle, who met me at a set of beautiful golden gates. They opened before me and as I entered inside, he escorted me into a courtyard. I could see the new Jerusalem and the temple that is yet to descend out of the clouds onto the Earth. It was beautiful and glorious. We walked past the Outer Courts and into the Holy Place and I could see Jesus seated on the Mercy Seat. I started to speak with Him. Jesus had reminded me about an earlier conversation defining our role as sons. When Father sees us, He sees royalty.

As I was reminded of this I noticed in the natural, that beautiful purple leaves and flowers were starting to blossom, while others were fading. I noticed that many of the trees had sprouted lush green foliage; however, as I looked closer, I saw that some trees appeared as if half of the newly formed leaves were dead. The leaves were turning brown and crumbling, and what was more astonishing was that it wasn't just one tree; there were many trees on my journey. Completely perplexed by this being the beginning of Spring, I asked the Father what the meaning of this was.

He often communicated with me through natural occurrences, and this instance was no exception. In the natural world, the leaves were withering due to rainwater that had been mixed with salt from the ocean, causing them to decay. However, the Father revealed a deeper symbolic meaning behind this phenomenon and explained it to me:

> *This is the condition of the church; the church is half dead inside. Spiritually, the body is half dead; the church is dying inside; many are lacking in fire and zeal, and they are lacking in purpose to pursue the heart of the Father and the things of His Kingdom.*

This made me very sad, and all I could pray was, "May it never be; revive us."

He continued to explain spiritual truths with natural means, and said:

> *The purple fading flowers and leaves represent the crowns of those who are lost and mixing in*

*with the world, their crowns fading and with it their authority and desire for intimacy with God.*

In love, Jesus cautioned me not to be like them. He said:

*My child, you are commissioned to a higher calling and will grow into it in due time. You are so loved, even beyond what you can fathom in your current state. Your continued growth in the desire for more intimacy and revelation is a delight to My heart and excites Me. I yearn for more of you, just like your spirit thirsts for more of Me; I rejoice when you are near My presence. Seek Me wholeheartedly, and you will never be disappointed, My dear child. You are My beloved, My Bride, My most cherished creation. I desire that My fire, My love, My spirit dwells richly within you.*

I saw a vision of white flower petals falling off cherry blossom trees. It looked like snow was falling. Father said, *"I have given you this position and this seat to go forth and harvest the nations."*

On another occasion, I was taken into a vision and saw myself wearing a long white mantle with a hood. It was twilight, and I was standing atop the peak of a mountain. The wind was whipping the cape behind me, and as I squinted to see ahead, I noticed a narrow path. I started walking onward and could see around me a hedge of protection and the angels of the Lord. Jesus said:

*The new season continues. Come out of the cave and behold the marvelous wonders of the Lord. My child, for some time, you have felt hollow and empty, And your religious worship offerings and partnership were led out of your soul realm; note how you felt hollow and empty. That emptiness you felt was the lack of My grace, the lack of My Spirit, and the lack of My release for you to do what I would like you to do. There are many in the body that operate in this way. Child, it is this emptiness that leads to a lifeless church, the church that is half-dead inside.*

*I have transplanted you to a place where you can serve, where you will be used, the place where you will grow, the place where you will be nurtured in all things that have been written in your scroll for this season shall be released. If you listen and obey, this is the season of advancement, the season of awakening. Follow My voice, and you will never be let down.*

*My son, do not be swept up in the world's hypocrisy. Many are quick to deceive My children. Many have been deceived and walk in crooked ways. Many will never know Me, so they don't know the sound of My voice, they don't yield to*

*My call, and they have never known Me. Stand firm in your faith because days are coming when it will be tested. Sometimes, My child, you must make yourself the least important one in the room, but you are always important to Me!*

In another encounter with the realms of Heaven and the depths of the Father's eternal love, I found myself in a vivid experience that felt like I was free-falling through the skies. The sensation was overwhelming as if I were plummeting at a thousand miles per hour. Suddenly, the descent ended with a tremendous splash—I had plunged into the midst of an endless ocean.

I swam under the water and took notice of many big and beautiful fish. The colors were beyond what the human experience can rightly categorize or express in words. I saw a large angel fish before me and grabbed ahold of its dorsal fin. As this fish swam a great distance, it pulled me towards the surface. As it swam up to the surface, it started to swim in circles faster and faster. I started to lose my grip and ultimately was flung out of the water and onto an island. I landed on the sand, and before me stood Jesus and his disciple John the Beloved, sitting there waiting for me. Jesus showed me a white crystal, and power flowed into and from it. I knew how God had created crystals, gems, and stones to be power sources for galaxies, societies, and infrastructures. I was then shown people on Earth who had taken these heavenly creations, perverted their meaning, and used and fashioned them into creations that were used in the practices of idolatry. They were worshipping the created thing rather than the one who created it for good use. Jesus spoke to me and said, *"Rest, this is a season of learning to rest. There is a predestined or appointed time for everything created by the Father."*

I was shown the timing of my going to learn with LifeSpring's Facilitator's Training,[5] and all the revelation in that year was preplanned by the Father to enrich my spiritual growth into what I was called to do for Him; the school was a school of the prophetic that He had planned to use to springboard me forward. Holy Spirit had explained there is a time and season for all things and led me to Ecclesiastes 3, which speaks to the appointed seasons and purposes under Heaven.

## Things to Come

As I sat down to spend time with the Father one day, I heard Him say, *"Settle into My timing child and all things will be revealed."*

---

[5] LifeSpring has a Facilitator Training Program to learn how to cleanse your generations and function in the Courts of Heaven. Visit RonHorner.com/lsom/ftp

I was then taken into a revelatory encounter. I was in Heaven, standing on the peak of a snowcapped mountain with Jesus. This place was called "the Mountain of the Lord." I could see a cloud cover below and all of the heavenly realm; below the clouds, I could see the Earth, and it was like a tiny blue pebble; the Lord had me gaze to see how minuscule my worries and cares are from Heaven's perspective.

He explained that when the devil tempted Him by taking Him to the highest mountain on Earth and offering all the kingdoms of the world, none of it could compare to the splendor and majesty of what I was witnessing. Moreover, everything already belonged to the Lord.

Suddenly, a massive pelican appeared and soared past us. We mounted its back, and it carried us just above the rivers of living water flowing through Heaven. After landing in a verdant grassy knoll surrounded by a lush forest, I noticed a staircase descending from the mountain.

As we followed the stairs, we arrived at a serene beach beside shimmering water. Before us appeared four radiant gates of light, each opening simultaneously. Though they seemed to provide different entry points, they all led to the same magnificent destination, the Throne Room.

I ran to the Father and climbed into His lap like a small child, saying, "I'm sorry, Lord. I've been caught up in my own thoughts and flesh lately. Please forgive me. Can you show me the current wellspring?"

In that moment, I saw a fountain in the Throne Room and eagerly ran toward it. In the spirit, I had a vision of myself seated and soaking in His presence, listening to worship music. The Father then summoned my angels to draw near to me. I could clearly see portions of them, particularly one named Phillip. He appeared strong and burly, with a neatly trimmed black-brown beard. He wore body armor and a flowing cloak, exuding a sense of readiness and protection.

Lilly came up and was standing next to him, her hair in a braid that extended around both sides of her head, almost like a crown and then down in the back. Her stature was smaller, almost looking like a teenage daughter next to Phillip in size.

Also wearing armor and a tunic of sorts, I saw Phillip grab a bottle out of this utility belt or sash of some sort that was positioned on his chest. He uncorked it and poured something into the fountain—three drops of this fluid. It was pink. I just heard the words, *"The Father's love."* As I gazed down, I saw my reflection, and it was as though I looked just like Jesus. The Father spoke tenderly, saying, *"My beloved son."*

In the water, an image appeared—myself, my wife, and my family standing together, hand in hand, in perfect unity.

It felt as if we were standing on a bluff or hill, overlooking a breathtaking new horizon. The atmosphere was warm, bright, and full of beauty.

I noticed what appeared to be movement—furniture being relocated—and sensed that a significant transition was approaching. I then saw a vision of us as a family, kneeling in a circle in what seemed to be a living room or den. We were holding hands, praying together, unified in faith and purpose.

I was then shown quick glimpses of what looked like different things: ministering opportunities, encounters, music and worship, art, and creativity flowing through the new place. Then I saw myself and my bride on a honeymoon or private trip—just us, then an image further in the future being an old man with my beautiful old lady by my side and a gathering of young children around us—grandchildren. Then another vision where the grandchildren were even older and advanced in years with those children's children and then praying with and for each other, and us watching as one was leading a worship service.

My angel said, "Many generations of righteousness will flow from your loins." As he said that, the Father's hand came heavy on my left shoulder as He said:

*Be still, My child, all is well with you. Trust in Me; I have got you, and if you will put your full faith in Me the miracles will be limitless; I am a limitless God; take the limits off your faith, let the doubts melt away, give Me your all and I will give you nothing less than My best.*

Then He said,

> *I love you; you are so important to Me, there will never be another you, Jeremy. Do all that I have commanded without wavering, and you will never be without what you need when in need. All of My promises are 'yes' and 'amen.'*

I then saw a rainbow wrapping around me, His promises and rainbow glory. I wept and said, "You truly know My heart." He told me that my current assignment still needed to be completed and to continue with it until the new assignment is given.

Suddenly, men clothed in white appeared—Jonah, Noah, Job, and Malachi. They introduced themselves and said they had come to welcome me into the assignments of pioneering for this new season. One of them placed a scroll into my heart, symbolizing the revelation being imparted, and they laid their hands on my shoulder as a sign of commissioning.

Then, the Father's voice resonated with authority and love, saying, *"Go forth and prosper."*

*¹ My faith shelters my soul continually in Yahweh. Why would you say to me: "Run away while you can!*

*Fly away like a bird to hide in the mountains for safety. ² For your enemies have prepared a trap for you! Can't you see them hiding in their place of darkness and shadows? They're set against all those who live upright lives. ³ What can the righteous accomplish when truth's pillars are destroyed and law and order collapse?"⁴ Yet Yahweh is never shaken— He is still found in His temple of holiness, reigning as King Yahweh over all. He closely watches and examines everything man does. With a glance, His eyes examine every heart, for His heavenly rule will prevail over all. ⁷ But remember this: Yahweh is the Righteous One who loves justice, and every godly one will gaze upon His face! (Psalms 11:1-4, 7, TPT)*

*¹ Wisdom has built herself a palace upon seven pillars to keep it secure. ⁴ "Whoever wants to know me and receive my wisdom. ⁶ Lay aside your simple thoughts and leave your paths behind. Agree with my ways, live in my truth, and you will find righteousness." ¹⁰ The starting point for acquiring wisdom is to be consumed with awe as you worship Yahweh. To receive the revelation of the Holy One, you must come to the one who has living understanding. ¹¹ Wisdom will extend your life, making every year more fruitful than the one before. ¹² So it is to your advantage to be wise. But to ignore the counsel of wisdom is to invite trouble into your life. (Proverbs 9:1, 4, 6, 10-12, TPT)*

# Chapter 6
# Exhortations of the Father

One morning, I woke up and made my way to the living room to spend time with the Father. Sitting on the couch, I began reading the Word, seeking peace. On this particular day, I realized I had been focusing more on the trials I was facing and what seemed to be going wrong rather than on the things that were going right, or on the sweet face of the Savior.

I have found that when life overwhelms us, if we tune our ears to hear from Heaven, the exhortations of the Father and the comfort of the Holy Spirit will always bring us back to reality. As I sat licking my wounds, the Father's voice rang out loud and clear in my spirit, and this is what He said:

*Do not try so hard to do things in your own strength; lean on Me. My son, do not succumb to the tormenting spirits that surround you. Press into My glorious presence, for it is there you shall be hidden and protected from the frequencies of the Earth realm and the soot of the ungodly. The sons of disobedience will yet be devoured like coal in a furnace, yet the sons of My Kingdom will thrive and be blessed.*

He led me into the Word to confirm that what I was hearing was, in fact, His voice speaking in that moment.

*In that day His burden will be taken off your shoulders, and His yoke off your neck. Indeed, the yoke will be broken because of fatness. (Isaiah 10:27, TLV)*

*Then He responded to me by saying, 'This is the word of ADONAI to Zerubbabel saying: "Not by might, nor by power, but by My Ruach!" says ADONAI-TZVA'OT. (Zechariah 4:6, TLV)*

The Father said:

*Stir up your faith, child! Today will be a glorious day. You are My beloved son. You are most valued and most adored. Do not let sin convict your heart, press on and press into Me. Let your heart be repentant when you err. Allow it to be supple and full of love, not calloused and full of venom. Do not be rife with worry, but be filled with grace, love, peace and mercy that surpasses human understanding; let My love transform and overflow you. Do not be devoured by the distractions that surround you, step into My glorious presence and allow them to melt away.*

*Caring for what I care for is intimacy. It is tender devotion and love. By displaying the character attributes of My heart to others in intercession, you are engaging in all aspects of intimacy with Me. Spend your days and nights in My arms, and harm will never come to you.*

Holy Spirit said:

*You are being made fertile soil, the Lord can plant in. You will bear good fruit.*

He continued to instruct me and said:

*Be self-forgetting, He is stripping away things that don't belong. All these things that you were growing through have an expected end, one that is much greater than any you can fathom. Do not allow yourself to become discouraged but stand firm in the faith knowing that the Lord your God is with you. Know that it is He who is doing this good work in you. Know that it is He who is drawing near to him, that you will know His heart and emulate the fullness of all His love. Show such love towards all His children, both those in the Kingdom of light and those who are wandering in darkness. It is through this overpowering love that many will be delivered from bondage into the promises of God. Yield yourself to the working of the Spirit in your life and allow every perfect work*

*of the Father to bear its roots within you that you*
*may overcome by the blood of the lamb and the*
*word of His testimony.*

## Father is Always Watching

In another engagement with the Father that week, He spoke to me of the separation I felt from Him. This was a time when I was wrestling to overcome patterns of self-doubt, depreciating thoughts and an orphan mindset.

During this season as I was being delivered. I had moments where I felt as if He was so far away. His words echoed in the dark hallways of My mind, and I felt His presence as He whispered to me:

*Oh, dear child, I am delighted when you seek*
*My face. Be kind, comforting, and a good steward*
*of your home and resources; all your valiant efforts*
*shall be rewarded and do not go unnoticed. I am*
*always watching you, you are so beloved; there is*
*nothing that can separate you from My love; I am*
*so proud of you. Press forward! Things might not*
*always make sense to you. Sometimes, you might*
*feel as if you were going straight for a dead end,*
*but in reality, I am making a new way. The path*
*may look like a detour, but it will lead you onto a*
*righteous path by which you overcome obstacles.*
*If you follow Me, this way is one by which you go*

*around the mountains, and you will overcome in the natural. This process may seem like it might be taking longer, but remember, I am a timeless & limitless God. There is no time in eternity. What seems like a long time on the Earth is but the blink of an eye in Heaven.*

As I turned to the Word to find confirmation and comfort, these verses seemed to echo the Father's sweet voice.

*Consider what I am saying, for the Lord will give you understanding in everything. (2 Timothy 2:7, TLV)*

*For those who live according to the flesh set their minds on the things of the flesh, but those who live according to the Spirit, the things of the Spirit. For to be carnally minded is death, but to be spiritually minded is life and peace. (Romans 8:5-6)*

*If then you were raised with Christ, seek those things which are above, where Christ is, sitting at the right hand of God. Set your mind on things above, not on things on the Earth. (Colossians 3:1-2)*

### Love As He Loves

In a later engagement, Heaven's instruction reaffirmed Father's love. Heaven said:

*Do not let the barrenness of joyless people affect you. Allow the peace of God and the joy of your Lord to overflow from the Father's heart through you. Allow His joy to flood those who oppose you and destroy their walls like a torrent of water. The tidal waves of the Father's love will crush all obstacles. Do not be dismayed by the ones stuck in the prison of Earth's soiling frequencies, but like Colossians 3:1, rise up and allow your spirit to manifest the frequencies of Heaven. The highs of the highest Heavens are no match for the lows of the Earth's chasms.*

As these words were spoken to me, the Lord brought to mind the story of Elkanah and Hannah from 1 Samuel 1, encouraging me to draw strength from their example.

Jesus then said,

*Don't allow the hurt of others to influence your heart, child. Those who don't know Me, or aren't firm in their identity, falter and can lash out at others in ways that can impact hearts and deter destinies. Do not allow undelivered places in those around you to ignite the fire of the tongue or inflict wounds on your heart. Your heart is the wellspring of life; it is the place where My spirit dwells within you. If you trust in Me and leave your heart in My hands, I will never hurt it or break it but will shield it from the things of this realm that cause hate and harm.*

*Love as I love and have loved you. Be still in moments of trials and know I am by your side; do not allow the fallen princes and powers of darkness6 to deceive you into believing the lies they tell mankind. I will always be with you; I am always for you!*

*This is a season in which there will be tests, but you have been groomed for such a time as this; there is no giant that can withstand the wrath of the Lord sent against it. Remember the authority you possess in Christ as Christ is indwelling in you through the spirit of the Living God, Holy Spirit. No darkness can or will stand.7*

*There is a purpose for everything you have gone through and will go through; the worry and concern you possess for your wife and family is a trap. Stand steadfast in your faith: you are the king-priest! Your fervent prayer thwarts the attacks of the wicked one. His lies are sinister and unforgiving; He relentlessly accuses the sons and daughters of God, hoping to break their faith and break them down. Do not allow yourself to*

---

[6] Ephesians 6:12
[7] John 1:5

*succumb to these wimpy attacks. You are in Christ. Remember that your wife and family are in Christ.*

*Stay in prayer, stay in the Father's presence, continue to increase your intimacy with the Father, when you carry His presence darkness cannot come near. When you are in your own strength your weariness allows moments for the enemy to try and fire His darts and arrows.*

*Stay on guard, child of God, mount up your horses and prepare for war. Continue in the absorption of Kingdom truth. Allow your heart to be filled with My joy that the swelling of such goodness and wonder would radiate in the lives of those around you and eclipse the frequencies that harm hearts and deter people from being free to experience the goodness God has intended for them.*

*Love unapologetically, relentlessly pursuing what is good and pure. Be released to experience all the glorious riches the Father has intended for you.*

# Chapter 7
# Surrendering to His Love

During a season of profound growth in my faith, I walked down roads filled with significant challenges. This period, spanning from 2020 to 2021, was one of transformation as the Lord led us geographically, much like He did for many in the Body of Christ during the COVID pandemic.

As we began the journey of becoming rooted in a new church home, my heart ached as I watched my wife struggle to adjust. As a husband, it was difficult to see her wrestle with the process. She was eager to serve in the ministries she felt called to yet was also healing from the emotional and spiritual wounds caused by past experiences with religion and control.

As I watched my wife's crushing and pressing, I felt weakness watching her process. As a feeler, often I would take on bearing her emotional burdens. My heart would ache as a husband who desired to help her receive freedom from things troubling her. Change was becoming easier for me to tolerate in my walk, but at this time I sought too much to be the fixer of her problems. I kept getting in God's way. My earthly resolutions could do her no good. As I came to the end of myself all I could do was seek the Father to hear his voice on how I should respond. The Father spoke and said:

*I told you, My son, this is her comeback season. Let her catch fire. Do not weigh yourself down with anxious thoughts, for [together] you have a high calling. Things will happen that will bring new revelation and knowledge to those who know Me not, and the power of God will be unleashed in magnified glory.*

*Be still and know, I am for you; this is the season of your departure from self-condemnation to identity as a son. As you grow in sonship, intimacy will follow. I know your heart's desires for I am He who placed them within you. It is I who calls you to Myself; although you don't yet fully understand, you will come into the fullness and understanding that the door is unlocked. You have knocked; now, it is time to step through it and seize your inheritance. Angry people give full vent to their mouths but are not ready to receive when the wise repent and try to reconcile.*

*My son, be still of heart. Do not be moved by past pain and trauma or the actions of others. Abandon selfish desires and motives and soak deeply in My love; My presence will overwhelm*

*and overcome all hurts and contusions the earthen
frequencies cause. Still your mind and heart. Focus
on My face and My love for you. At My right hand,
you will find what you desire.*

As I dove into the scriptures on my heart it echoed
Father's words.

*²² And He has taught you to let go of the lifestyle of
the ancient man, the old self-life, which was
corrupted by sinful and deceitful desires that spring
from delusions. ²³ Now it's time to be made new by
every revelation that's been given to you. ²⁴ And to be
transformed as you embrace the glorious Christ-
within as your new life and live in union with him!
For God has re-created you all over again in his
perfect righteousness, and you now belong to Him in
the realm of true holiness.*

*²⁶ But don't let the passion of your emotions lead you
to sin! Don't let anger control you or be fuel for
revenge, not for even a day. ²⁷ Don't give the
slanderous accuser, the Devil, an opportunity to
manipulate you!*

*²⁹ And never let ugly or hateful words come from your
mouth, but instead let your words become beautiful
gifts that encourage others; do this by speaking words
of grace to help them. ³⁰ The Holy Spirit of God has*

*sealed you in Jesus Christ until you experience your full salvation. So never grieve the Spirit of God or take for granted His holy influence in your life. (Ephesians 4:22-24, 26-27, 29-30, TPT)*

Holy Spirit said:

> *You are learning self-control.*

*⁴ As a result of this, Jesus has given you magnificent promises that are beyond all price so that through the power of these tremendous promises we can experience partnership with the divine nature, by which you have escaped the corrupt desires that are of the world.*

*⁵ So devote yourselves to lavishly supplementing your faith with goodness, and to goodness add understanding, ⁶ and to understanding add the strength of self-control, and to self-control add patient endurance, and to patient endurance add godliness, ⁷ and to godliness add mercy toward your brothers and sisters, and to mercy toward others add unending love. ⁸ Since these virtues are already planted deep within, and you possess them in abundant supply, they will keep you from being inactive or fruitless in your pursuit of knowing Jesus Christ more intimately. (2 Peter 1:4-8, TPT)*

Holy Spirit said,

*This is the way, My child, walk in it, walk in love, let your light shine before men and let your deeds glorify the Father in Heaven. His light provides a multitude of things, but it's most powerful attribute is the unfailing love of the Father. The instinctive overflow of every molecule in the human body resonates at the frequency of this love. As the living water flows through you others will feel the presence of Glory all around. Do not hold back from the full expression of the Father's undying devotion for all His children, 'to live is Christ to die is gain.'*

He brought to mind this scripture:

*So also, you have sorrow now; but I will see you again, and your heart will rejoice, and no one will take your joy away from you. (John 16:22, TLV)*

# Chapter 8
## Deep Calls to Deep

The process of spiritual growth—of breaking free from what no longer serves us and maturing in our faith—is both challenging and rewarding. The Word of God assures us that salvation comes freely by believing in Jesus. However, the anointing requires a different process—a cost to be paid. In the following chapter, I recount part of my journey, sharing the dialogues and encounters with Heaven that provided encouragement as I was transformed into a new wineskin. I hope that as you read, your heart will be drawn into a deeper understanding and experience of the Father's love.

None of our situations are unique or untenable. Heaven has your back! We are beloved children of the Most High. If we are facing trials and persecutions, it's because we are walking closer and closer to Jesus every day. Be encouraged, keep pressing on and straighten your crown of victory; our Papa adores and delights in you! You are HIS beloved!!!

*And let us not be weary in well doing: for in due season, we shall reap, if we faint not. (Galatians 6:9)*

*Now we know that all things work together for good*
*for those who love God, who are called according to*
*His purpose. (Romans 8:28, TLV)*

## His Love Conquers Us

As I was going through a time of intense pressing and persecution, I was taught about the deep love of the Father that comforts in the midst of hardship. I learned that sometimes what we think is warfare is actually the Father dealing with our hearts. The Great Gardener prunes away our dead branches so we can bear fruit. As I was learning to allow his love to soothe my broken places, I was taken into an encounter where I was taught of His love. On this September morning in 2021, I learned a very important lesson—how to love beyond limits. The Holy Spirit spoke these words in the midst of my pain:

> *Love in the midst of persecution. Be about the*
> *business of the Father and not of the flawed, vile,*
> *and fruitless thinking of the Earth. Bitterness and*
> *rage have no place among My flock, but love,*
> *compassion, grace, and mercy are the tools of*
> *warriors skilled in the art of love and peacemaking.*
> *Be still and know love shall rule your heart, love is*
> *of the Kingdom, love is the key to peace.*

As I opened my Bible to find comfort in the Word, I was taken to the Beatitudes and subsequent scriptures:

*Blessed are those who have been persecuted for the sake of righteousness, for theirs is the Kingdom of Heaven. 'Blessed are you when people revile you and persecute you and say all kinds of evil against you falsely, on account of Me. Rejoice and be glad, for your reward in Heaven is great! For in the same way, they persecuted the prophets who were before you.' (Matthew 5:10-12, TLV)*

*You have heard that it was said, 'You shall love your neighbor and hate your enemy.' But I tell you, love your enemies and pray for those who persecute you so that you may be children of your Father in Heaven. He causes His sun to rise on the evil and the good and sends rain on the righteous and the unrighteous. (Matthew 5:43-45, TLV)*

*Therefore, be perfect, just as your Father in Heaven is perfect. (Matthew 5:48, TLV)*

As I continued to wrestle through this new stage of growth and development, I heard the Lord say:

*My son, be still and know My love for you is extravagant! In this season, you are going to witness mighty things, you are going to witness moves of God that are unparalleled. The things you have seen in the last season will pale in comparison to the signs, wonders and miracles yet*

71

*to come. This process (refinement) you are going through, although it is painful and crippling, it is very necessary for what is yet to come, the greater things which I have for you to walk in require a greater level of holiness and purity and infallibility. it can only be achieved through full submission, by allowing the Holy Spirit to be your guide in all things. Yield to My perfect will for your life, and all things will be well; all things will prosper by My Almighty hand. I just ask that you trust Me and trust the process. I will give you strength to overcome.*

The following scripture was brought to mind:

*I know all about your deeds and your toil and your patient endurance, and that you cannot bear those who are evil. You have tested those who call themselves emissaries and are not and have found them to be liars. You have perseverance and have endured for My name's sake, and you have not grown weary. (Revelation 2:2-3, TLV)*

Again, I heard the Holy Spirit speaking to me. He said:

*Child, My winds are blowing in your life. The chaff is being blown off like dust blown off an old book; the full cover of the world's devices is being stripped away and exposing you to walk in a fully surrendered identity of sonship. Oh, My son, be still and allow yourself to be in the quiet place of rest, the Secret Place for there you will find refreshment and rest for your soul.*

*When you continuously exist in a place or striving and do not take appropriate rest, you weary your soul. It is in these moments that the enemy will seek a crack to try and wear down your defensive tactics and protocols of living a spirit-filled, redeemed, and yielded life. My heart is to see you blessed; My heart is to see you prosper. It is not to see you clamoring for the things of the flesh that will never fulfill you.*

*I know the depths of the brokenness of your soul, and I am here to heal the sorrow. Give that which is painful into My hand, that I might heal it. I will restore the breaches and fix the gaps; I will mend the fences and destroy all that oppose you. You are My beloved child, and it breaks My heart to see your heart breaking. It breaks My heart to see you longing for that which will never satisfy the way that the love I wish to give you will.*

*Allow Me to pour out afresh on you today. Allow Me to stir the waters within you, the living water, that will revive your spirit, your soul and your flesh. The old things are passing away, and you'll be filled with new life, new joy, new peace, and more love than you can ever fathom.*

As I entered the Secret Place, I saw white sandy beaches before me, seagulls overhead and sailboats in the distance in the calm still waters. The cool, warm breeze of the winds of destiny blew on me, as they did, I noticed a book buried in the sand. The gusts of wind shifted the sand and more fully revealed this book.

I then saw Jesus walking with a few of the disciples and other men in white. He scooped the book out of the sand and held it out to me to receive it. I saw on it the words "Book of Destiny." As He opened the dust cover, the pages unfurled like a long scroll. It cascaded down the beach like a red carpet being rolled out. My eyes focused on one segment by my feet that said:

> *The stillness of God's Spirit, moving on the waters of your soul, will give you rest and refresh you. This is your inheritance as a son, be a steward of peace, live in the place of rest which is the glorious presence of the Father.*

As I searched the Word to confirm what I had heard, I was brought to Psalm 46:1 and 10.

> *¹ God is our refuge and strength. A very present help in trouble.*

> *¹⁰ Be still and know that I am God.*

## Worship the Pain Away

A few days later, as I was worshipping in the morning, I was transported to Heaven and found myself prostrate on my face before the Throne of the Lord. I was crying and repenting, heavy-hearted from being distant from the Father's loving embrace. At this time, I had been through a lot of trials but was not walking in the fullness of intimacy. My well was dry. I was irritable as I had neglected to be intentional to seek God amid the trials, and now it was taking a spiritual toll on me.

The Father grabbed me and held me with a loving embrace. As I continued to soak in the presence of the Lord, the Spirit of Holiness descended upon me. I saw some angels that had surrounded me, and they were digging and pulling things out of me that didn't belong. Holy Spirit told me that they were smiting forces of darkness that had come against me.

Suddenly, I saw a group of men in white linen coming up to pray over me. In the spirit, I recognized some of them from the great cloud of witnesses that surround us in Heaven. I had an understanding that one such saint was my brother who was in Heaven, Dana Robin. He had never been born in the natural as my mother had a miscarriage before conceiving me, but he was there with Jesus all the while. He traded into me an anointing called "The Favor and Blessing of the First Born." Heaven explained that since Dana was not born in the natural and would have been the first, I was robbed of this blessing. I was told that this would manifest in supernatural favor.

Another man approached, and I was introduced to Job. He was there to bless me with a gift that I understood as a covenant with my eyes that partnered with faithfulness to the wife given to a man by God.

Then I saw Isaiah and Jeremiah approaching. I could feel the amplification of the weighty Glory of Heaven bearing down on me. My body was heavy, as if I was plastered to the floor. Jeremiah laid his hands upon me and traded into me the weeping and crying of the Lord through intercession. Isaiah declared the prophetic gifting of reading and proclaiming the Word of the Lord over my life. As the encounter continued, more and more people gathered around me in Heaven.

A man in a cloak came towards me; it was Samuel the prophet. He handed me a staff and a horn of oil and told me he was here to trade into me "the discernment of being a Kingmaker" and knowledge of how to use that call appropriately as a prophet to anoint kings and leaders and rightfully so to cut down those who kingship was to be taken from at the Lord's direction.

King David appeared next and informed me he was there to bestow me with the gift of the heart of worship and a heart of being focused on the Lord and forsaking the world. He called this a process by which one can have a clean heart and a greater understanding of intimacy in worship.

Moses had appeared and laid hands on me, as he did, he spoke that he was imparting into me wisdom and knowledge of leadership. With him was Abraham, who also blessed me with his knowledge of what it means to be a friend of God. As the encounter ended, I lay in the presence of the Lord, weeping, awestruck and unable to move or speak.

I heard the Holy Spirit say, *"Seek greater intimacy with the Lord; only His presence will truly comfort you and restore you to what you have been called to move in!"*

As I attempted to compose myself and dive back into the Word of God, the following scriptures seemed to confirm so perfectly all I had just encountered and restore my soul.

> *You're my place of quiet retreat, and your wraparound presence becomes my shield as I wrap myself in your Word! (Psalms 119:114, TPT)*

> *Here I am, doing a new thing; Now it is springing up—do you not know about it? I will surely make a way in the desert, rivers in the wasteland. (Isaiah 43:19, TLV)*

> *23 Be renewed in the spirit of your mind 24 and put on the new self—created to be like God in true*

*righteousness and holiness. <sup>25</sup> So lay aside lying and*
*"each one of you speak truth with his neighbor," for*
*we are members of one another. <sup>26</sup> "Be angry, yet do*
*not sin." Do not let the sun go down on your anger,*
*<sup>27</sup> nor give the devil a foothold. <sup>28</sup> The one who steals*
*must steal no longer, instead he must work, doing*
*something useful with his own hands, so he may have*
*something to share with the one who has need.*

*<sup>29</sup> Let no harmful word come out of your mouth, but*
*only what is beneficial for building others up*
*according to the need, so that it gives grace to those*
*who hear it. <sup>30</sup> Do not grieve the Ruach ha-Kodesh of*
*God, by whom you were sealed for the day of*
*redemption. <sup>31</sup> Get rid of all bitterness and rage and*
*anger and quarreling and slander, along with all*
*malice. <sup>32</sup> Instead, be kind to one another,*
*compassionate, forgiving each other just as God in*
*Messiah also forgave you. (Ephesians 4:23-32, TLV)*

## The Best is Yet to Come

On another morning, as I sat in prayer, I heard the Holy
Spirit speaking to me, wooing me, and pouring out His love
on me. The beauty of his words was timely and sweet as
honey to my ears. It was a time of intense crushing for me as
my identity was being refined and formed, but there were

moments I felt so broken I wanted to quit. As he spoke, the words melted off the weight of the world. He said:

*The beauty of what is yet to come is still to be manifest. The pruning season leads to an abundance of fruit not barrenness. Rise up, child of God, for the best is yet to come.*

In a vision, I saw meadows filled with trees. I heard Heaven say:

*These meadows are meadows of fruit; the good fruit being bared and the saplings that were planted that will bear more fruit in a later season. The field is no longer fallow; they are well tended. The harvest is at hand.*

*My son, this is a season you will learn of the holiness of God in such a magnificent and awesome way. Get ready to experience waves of His Glory that will bowl you over. Those you pray for will be wrecked beyond recognition. Limiting thought forms and strongholds in mind and heart will break when you pray.*

*All My Glory Carriers can manifest this power of My presence in prayer. Relationally, it is important to stay in the shadow of My wings, step out in faith, but be aware of stepping out on soulish desire versus the spirit's unction.*

*Be still knowing that I am with you, I am for you and will always be with you, through the fire, the flood waters, and the storm, when you are in My strength and walking in My spirit, they shall not overflow or overpower you. Be still and know that I am God, and you are My beloved son!*

# Chapter 9
# The Lord Who Affirms Us

On the morning of September 29, 2021, as I sat in my living room, I was taken into a vision where I found myself on the shores of eternity, sitting on the sands of time with Jesus. Together, we gazed out over the ocean, and in the distance, I saw the second heaven below. Jesus then asked if I wanted to see the farthest reaches of the galaxy. As He spoke, He began showing me the magnificent galaxies the Father had created—glorious beyond measure.

Afterward, I entered the Business Complex to meet with my business angels and receive instructions for the day. As I did, I began to hear the Father's voice. He said:

> *I want you to do something for Me today. Allow yourself to be submerged in My love; don't let the weight of the world rest on your shoulders. In My perfect love, there is no fear, no concern, no worry, only abundance of grace, mercy, and forgiveness.*

I saw a globe, and on the globe, there were small pockets of people standing, hands lifted in praise. This uprising of praise spread from small pockets to covering the whole globe. It was the Earth covered in people praising the Lord.

Heaven said:

*This is the evolution of the Earth as darkness flees and humanity/the Earth is washed in the Lord's light. Let your light shine, child; do not let devilish deceptions rule your thought life, commission your angels over your gates.*

Following the unction of the Holy Spirit, I commissioned the angels assigned to myself and my family to stand guard over our eye, ear, heart, and mind gates in the natural and supernatural realms. I asked if there was anything specific the angels needed to be equipped with and was informed that there was. To my surprise, the items were:

- Dark frequency-dampening earmuffs. These were a tool the angels could use to filter evil frequencies out from our ear gates and, in essence, were a defensive tool that benefited those they were co-laboring with.

- The angels also needed invisibility cloaks and binoculars.

As I asked the Father to release these items to our angels, the Lord took both my hands in his hands. He pulled me close and said, *"Beloved, you are so wonderful, My dear child; I am so proud of you; I love you. You are so beautifully created in My likeness and image."*

I said, "I don't always feel that way." It was honest but at the time I was not walking in the fullness of my true identity as a son. In His great love, He held me closer, reassured me and said, *"This is a season of explosion of grace and growth."*

With tears in my eyes, I replied, "Sometimes I feel far from you and rejected."

Jesus said to me, *"You may be rejected by people, but you will always be affirmed & accepted by God."*

John, the Beloved, showed up and said, "Why is your face so downcast? You are beloved! An overcomer!"

As He laid his hand on my shoulder, I could feel the presence of Heaven and electricity flowing through me and was told I was receiving the *overcomers anointing.* As I came out of the vision, I heard the Lord say that He loves when I play music for Him. He asked me to go to the piano and play a song I had written for Him. As I played, I wept in the Glory of His sweet presence. The Holy Spirit brought this scripture to mind:

*[10] We pray that you would walk in the ways of true righteousness, pleasing God in every good thing you do. Then you'll become fruit-bearing branches,*

*yielding to his life, and maturing in the rich experience of knowing God in his fullness! [11] And we pray that you would be energized with all his explosive power from the realm of his magnificent glory, filling you with great hope. [12] Your hearts can soar with joyful gratitude when you think of how God made you worthy to receive the glorious inheritance freely given to us by living in the light. [13] He has rescued us completely from the tyrannical rule of darkness and has translated us into the Kingdom realm of his beloved Son. [14] For in the Son all our sins are canceled, and we have the release of redemption through his very blood. (Colossians 1:10-14, TPT)*

On another occasion, I sat and listened to the Father's affirmations as they guided me through rough terrain. As I sat to write down the words, He spoke. This was the encouragement I received:

*Do not grow weary and do not grow faint but be filled with compassion and tender hearted, My son. Your burdens are eased when you rely on Me to carry them. Do not strive in your flesh, for you will become tiresome and weary, but in Me, you will find the true rest that your spirit craves and the nourishment your soul needs to be sustained. It is found only within My glorious presence. Rest well in Me, My son.*

The Holy Spirit brought this scripture to mind:

*But they who wait for ADONAI will renew their strength. They will soar up with wings as eagles. They will run, and not grow weary. They will walk, and not be faint. (Isaiah 40:31, TLV)*

The Father continued:

> *The anxiety you are feeling is the soul's desire for rest. The only remedy is more of Me, My son, more of My Spirit, more of My presence. This is a season to press in. There is a harvest to be gathered, but when the workers and laborers are paralyzed by fear and anxiety, the enemy will sneak in and overwhelm them with lies and false thoughts. It is these lies that deceive and debilitate; when your foundation is rock solid in Me, protected by Me and enshrouded in My love, none of these earthly frequencies and fallen tactics can prevail. You need to press in when your fuel tank is low. Seek Me. Call out to Me and worship in spirit and in truth and I will refresh your weariness. Life will come to your dry bones, and your desert places will overflow with the waters of life-giving power in Christ. Come to Me when you are heavy laden. I will give you rest.*

The Holy Spirit brought this scripture to mind:

*⁶ Be anxious for nothing, but in everything by prayer and supplication, with thanksgiving, let your requests be made known to God; ⁷ and the peace of God, which surpasses all understanding, will guard your hearts and minds through Christ Jesus. (Philippians 4:6-7)*

Father said:

*My son, be still in Me, and I will give you rest; I know the desires of your heart; they are only found when you seek Me and let Me in; When I knock, ask Me full of faith and expect the goodness of God to prevail in every situation. Remember to add to your rest quotient; the world says go, but in order to truly press forward, you must press into My presence, press in to press on. Striving in your own effort leads to stress and frustration. Do not buy into those lies. You will receive a double portion for your obedience to finding My presence as your resting place.*

*Be refreshed in the presence of the Lord; He is the king of Glory whose love is vast as the sea, pausing in His presence to hear His beloved voice restores the soul. It gives strength to the weak and refreshment to the weary. Lean into the Father's love when you are feeling raw, and He will help you to find the true rest and abundance of love that your heart craves at its deepest levels.*

*Stash yourself in Me; don't allow your love for the things of God to grow dim, to wax cold; allow your spirit to be ignited and seek after the Kingdom purpose deposited deep within your spirit. Detest what is evil but hate no one involved in it, for the love embodied in My light will draw those in lawlessness out of dark places.*

Then, Holy Spirit spoke to me and said, *"New levels are coming; today is the beginning of that expansion season. Be still. Don't eat the apple of the Garden of Eden."*

Instantly, I went into a vision of my heart being open for surgery, and the Lord had poured in different colored oil, which symbolized the Seven Spirits of the Lord.

*² I will go before you and make crooked places straight. I will shatter bronze doors and cut through iron bars. ³ I will give you treasures of darkness and hidden riches of secret places, so you may know that I am ADONAI, the God of Israel, who calls you by your name. (Isaiah 45:2-3, TLV)*

# Chapter 10

# For Every Time There Is a Purpose

This chapter contains a series of encounters and love notes from the Father. His nature is to help us to grow into the fullness of all He has for us, but the cost to know Him deeply and fully is immense. Every person who intends to walk closely with the Lord undergoes a process, seasons of pruning and refinement, seasons of training, and moments when the Holy Spirit is their only teacher in the wilderness.

Jesus did this, and after His forty days in the wilderness, there was an explosion of the manifestation and power of God in His ministry. If you are in such a season, lean into the fire, lean into the Father's heart. Weep in His lap and pour your love on Him. Praise Him and worship Him through the pain. Praise Him and worship Him through the blessings. There is no better treasure than when He walks into the room, and His presence makes us strong in weakness. As you read about the seasons journeying through such encounters, remember that Heaven is at hand. You only need to seek Him to find Him.

# Seasons of Testing

On the morning of August 4th, 2021, I was greeted by the following message from Father in my personal prayer time.

> *You are My beloved and dear child. Do not let yourself get pounded by the frequencies of the Earth realm that come knocking at the door. Jesus is calling, and He is knocking. All those who answer the call will be saved from the things that are coming upon the Earth right now.*

Jesus began to speak and said:

> *The enemy and his camp are running wild. They are mad. Their plans are continually foiled by the sons and daughters of God who are standing in their authority. Resist temptation, every trap, every trickery, and stand strong. Beloved one, know the Father's Glory. The Holy Spirit is richly and deeply embedded within you. He will lead you and guide you into all wisdom and all truth and guard you against all hypocrisy. Many think the Father is slow in keeping His promises. They feel unloved. Some feel unworthy and feel cast aside.*
>
> *In this season, you'll notice an uptick in some of the strategies that the enemy has used to put a death grip upon the children of God who are walking in disobedience. Those who are*

*disconnected from the Father's heart are those who are far from knowing the truth and the life in the way of Christ Jesus.*

*Beloved, you are called to restore such people to Glory. You must minister to their hearts and sow seeds of the Father's great love.*

*It is in this season you will begin to preach and prophesy love into the lives of many. Do not let your own love grow cold. Seek the Father in the depths of His intimacy so you can pour it out continually into the lives of all you meet. The best deliverance strategy Is the Father's love - one touch and all chains and bondages will fall away. Be still and know that I am with you always!!*

The Holy Spirit brought this scripture to mind:

*[18] If the world hates you, you know that it hated Me before it hated you. [19] If you were of the world, the world would love its own. Yet because you are not of the world, but I chose you out of the world, therefore the world hates you. [20] Remember the word that I said to you, 'A servant is not greater than his master.' If they persecuted Me, they will also persecute you. If they kept My word, they will keep yours also.*

*[21] But all these things they will do to you for My name's sake, because they do not know Him who sent*

*Me. ²² If I had not come and spoken to them, they would have no sin, but now they have no excuse for their sin. ²³ He who hates Me hates My Father also. ²⁴ If I had not done among them the works which no one else did, they would have no sin; but now they have seen and also hated both Me and My Father. ²⁵ But this happened that the word might be fulfilled which is written in their law, 'They hated Me without a cause.'*

*²⁶ 'But when the Helper comes, whom I shall send to you from the Father, the Spirit of truth who proceeds from the Father, He will testify of Me. ²⁷ And you also will bear witness because you have been with Me from the beginning.' (John 15:18-27)*

As this encounter ended, the Father said, *"The world may hate you, but Yeshua and I love you!"*

## Seasons of Shaking

In a subsequent encounter with the Holy Spirit, my engagement started with a word of knowledge. Heaven said,

*A great shaking is taking place not just in your job, but in leadership too, as you are a part of a shaking in the global community.*

Instantly, I was taken into a vision of Jesus walking across the water. At this moment in time, I was fighting a war within my own home prayerfully. I was watching my wife in a battle with generational iniquities that caused self-doubt and played upon past hurts. Rejection tried to find a home within our souls, and we were continually warring to overcome fallen mindsets and walk in sonship.

During this time, we were both in a transition season. We had been taken from a place of church hurt and brought into a place of spiritual growth and healing. Our flesh cried out to run back to what was familiar, but our spirits knew we were to follow God obediently. As a husband and a man of prayer, it was my heart to fix the situation, but the Lord chastened me and led me to fight the only way that would work on my knees, interceding from the Secret Place.

In prayer, I was taken into a vision of an ocean called despair. I observed choppy waters underneath stormy twilight skies. The wakes grew in size as they swelled and crashed upon one another. In the distance I saw a man, it was Jesus walking across the deep waters. Adjacent to Him, I could see hands flailing, like one trying to tread water. Then I noticed a head bobbing under and back above the waters; it was a woman screaming for help. I saw Jesus walking towards her and realized this woman was my wife. I watched the Lord intently as He bent down and grabbed her hand. In one quick motion He had scooped her up so that she would not sink into the dark waters, and she stood valiantly next to him.

Jesus spoke to me and said,

*I want you to be still; I have this situation; you will not be leaving or going anywhere else. Be still and know I am God; I work all things for My Glory.*

He continued to speak and inform me that He was helping my wife through a personal growth process. He said, *"I have to break off hardened places that have given birth to fear and stubbornness to be able to fully use her."* As I listened to the sweet sound of his harmonious voice, I saw Heaven's righteous armies marching towards us. There were multitudes of warrior angels suited up for battle and marching in unison. They held their war clubs high and chanted, "JESUS, JESUS, JESUS" in one accord.

I saw other hosts of Heaven that were called "The Winds of Heaven" and "The Lightnings of God" descend in the front of this army and take their stances in a battle-ready positioning. The Lord mounted upon a white horse, the one known as faithful and true. There was a double-edged sword He had in his hand and a red sash around his waist. He grabbed me and helped me onto the back of the horse. I heard an angel say, *"He leads the multitude out into battle."*

I started to focus my attention on an object that came into view. It was a book that had been opened. As I looked to see more detail, I could see it looked old and thick. It had a leather cover and parchment pages, and it was open to the middle where the bindings were.

The book said, "Heaven marches on for who can stop the Lord Almighty...." I saw the book close, and the hands that held it were the Father's.

Father looked at me, and His gaze pierced me. His eyes were full of fiery love. His heart was ablaze with hopeful and fond thoughts of me and my family. I knew He had plans to prosper us and give us a future and a hope (Jeremiah 29:11).

## Seasons of Rejoicing

In another adventure into the realms of Heaven, I proceeded to sit quietly, waiting upon a visitation from the Lord. Autumn was in the air in the northeast, and as I joyously awaited the presence of the Holy Spirit, I was filled with delight and expectation. So sweetly, I felt His presence come into the room, and when He showed up, I was eager to hear what He had to tell me. He began:

> *This morning, I just want you to know how loved and adored you are. This is the new season you are entering into, a season of thankfulness and gratitude. This shall be a season of rejoicing, and a season of which you will witness all the former things are being made new. Not only will this*

*happen in your own life, but this will be a season in which renewal will come upon the Earth.*

As I looked out my window and into the realm of the spirit, I saw the leaves turning beautiful shades of red, orange, and yellow but also the barrenness of leaves that had fallen and branches that were bare.

The Father observing me said, *"It looks much like death as the leaves fall off the trees."* I nodded.

He continued and said:

*As things wither and die in preparation for the winter, in the spirit of this season, you will be cocooning as a caterpillar goes into hiding to become butterflies, so shall this be for you and My bride. This is the season of the preparation for the children of God and the Kingdom purposes that are being birthed. It is a season of rejoicing and a season of joy, a season of happiness, a season of freedom, a season of liberty, and a season of revival.*

*Take heed, My son, know this season is one that will lead to growth, maturity, and continued development of spiritual things. I am releasing the expansion of revelation knowledge that will bring you into a deeper hunger and passion for the things of the Kingdom of Heaven. Do not burden yourself with worry in this season. Do not tarry, thinking of all the things that you need to get done. Seek My rest over the chores and tasks life has for you. Concern yourself solely with seeking first the Kingdom of God resting in My glorious presence. Be refreshed and allow yourself to operate out of My refreshment. Today is a day of rejoicing and dancing; allow yourself to be submerged in My glorious love.*

As He spoke this, in the spirit, I saw myself on a tire swing. The swing was atop a cliff, and below was water. Excitedly, I swung higher and higher, launching out of the time and swan-diving headfirst into a lake of crystal blue water below.

The Holy Spirit spoke and said:

*The bliss and joy of the Lord shall guide you in these last days, although the land falls into darkness and famine, the Spirit of the Lord shall light your path as the noonday sun, be not afraid from the turmoil and disease you see all around for I will protect you, you and your flock oh mighty warrior, it is this day I have called you prophet to prophecy to the nations, you are the anointed of God, My power flows through you, by fervent prayer and laying of hands, you shall see healing manifest in greater ways in this year, that the name and Kingdom of Christ thy king will be lifted* up and glorified. Fear not, young prophet, for the Lord your God is with you wherever you go, no go forth and take back what is rightfully the inheritance of the Kingdom and win souls for Heaven.

This season of rejoicing and merriment will yield much celebration upon the Earth. In the heavenly places, there's more rejoicing and celebration than one could imagine.

During other times and seasons, the world's calendar conflicts with the times and seasons of Heaven's calendar. But be assured it is a time of celebration of newness of life. This is indeed the time of celebration of revival, for the celebration of the King returning will soon be at hand. Do not be confused or deluded by the hypocrisy of man. Much lawlessness still runs rampant upon the Earth. The enemy's camp still concocts many diabolical plans, as they still tirelessly try to execute atrocities upon the Earth. Know this: their plan is a plan of failure. They have already been judged, and the Father's righteous hand is against all who exalt themselves above his name. Do not pay mind to the media, do not pay mind to the news, do not pay mind to that which will seek to confuse. Do not pay mind to reports of disease, or reports of famine, but seek first the Kingdom of God. Set your mind on the Throne of Heaven and *lean not on your own understanding. Know that the Lord Himself will lead and guide those who trust in him. They will be untouched throughout all the darkness of the land. He is your light; He will light the way of your path.*

As I received further instructions, I was told:

*It's time to war against all the spirits that have been trying to attack you. An all-out offensive assault is being launched even as we speak. The righteous armies of Heaven are going to war on your behalf. New angels are being sent to partner and work with the angels assigned to you, as well as others who serve the Kingdom of God. There will be a reckoning in this season where lawlessness will be cast down, and righteous pillars for the Throne of God and I will be set up across the land.*

*Be a man driven by My Spirit, and My heart desires, not the desires of the flesh. For the desire of flesh is sin and death. Its temptation is a snare ready to take your words and emotions to foul places of deceit and treachery, but the flow of the Spirit is the life-giving essence of life that soothes, heals, and reforms the desires of the world into the fondness for the things of the Kingdom. Do not be a prophet ensnared by falsehood and blinded by the tribulation around but rise up as a fiery one.*

*Set ablaze the chaff and tares for the Glory of The Father.*

As this encounter ended, the Holy Spirit spoke to me scriptures that encouraged me:

*Call to Me, and I will answer you—I will tell you great and hidden things, which you do not know. (Jeremiah 33:3, TLV)*

*Now we know that all things work together for good for those who love God, who are called according to His purpose. (Romans 8:28, TLV)*

On another occasion, I stepped into Heaven and saw many waterfalls before me. They were beautiful, with the deepest hues of cyan and blue I had ever beheld. I could feel the essence of the Father radiating from them. The waterfalls changed color to reflect the colors of the rainbow. As I watched them pour out into a pool below, they became one body of water flowing in complete harmony. I had a knowing in my spirit that these were the waters of refreshing, the living waters. I saw angels taking cisterns, scooping up this water and bringing into the Earth, where they pour out the refreshing our heavenly Father desired to give to His children.

I heard Heaven say:

*There is an advance taking place in the realms of Heaven; the doors of old are closing, old mindsets are wasting away. There is much coming to nothing and much coming to ruin. As a Phoenix rises from the ashes, so the Spirit of the Lord will rise up and overcome the people of God. Salvations will increase, a new outpouring of the Father's love, and Holy Spirit will issue forth from His Throne of Grace.*

*New revelation will be poured out, and the host of Heaven, the angels, will be in an all-out war against the dark forces that seek to stop Kingdom advancement. The doors of the Father's best have been flung wide open; make way for the King of Glory to come in.*

As I listened to this, I was so amazed and in awe of what the Father was about to do. He handed me a key. I asked what it would unlock. He said, *"The Heart of Intercession."*

This was the key to intercession for the nations, to pray for His people. As I proceeded to use it, it unlocked the desires of the Father's heart that I would pray as He had instructed.

## Seasons of Humbling

One day, as I sat in my car watching rain pour down on the windshield. I felt as if Heaven was weeping with me. My heart was heavy at this time of my life. I was in a place of grieving over losses in my past, as well as in a state of transition. As my soul wallowed in its feelings and longing for what was no longer my portion, the presence of Heaven broke into my car, and the Holy Spirit's voice broke the silence. He said:

*As the rain pours, you will see the new thing sprout forth. This will be a season of humbling for you, in which your branches shall be pruned. The branches that will grow back in will be extended towards the sky in worship and bring in refreshing, reframing, and the rebuilding of the new foundation.*

As I listened intently yet apprehensively about going through a season of pruning, I saw a door open in the spirit. Behind this great door was a yellow ocean, and as I saw the waves crash upon the shore, the presence of Heaven crashed over me. Waves of the Father's Glory were bringing peace to my soul.

Heaven instructed me:

*Shed earthly knowledge, shed judgments, shed the old and step into the new. The realms of revelatory encounters are waiting for you to dive in. In order to access the greater realms of Heaven, you must be ready to leave behind the baggage of the past. My heart's desire is for you to spring*

*forward towards a new destination, towards the
light and through this new door.*

The Father enveloped me in His embrace, speaking
words that echoed in the depths of my soul:

*You are deeply loved, incredibly special, and of
utmost importance to Me. There's a high calling on
your life, and with it, comes a high price and great
sacrifice. Be still and soak in My love daily, My
presence will soothe and cleanse your soul
wounds. The pain of pruning will soon be gone,
and in its place will rest a purity that will be the
catalyst to break open the Heavens over the
personal ministry I will lead you in. This is not the
end of your race but merely a valley. Prepare your
heart and rend your garments to prepare yourself
for the mountain top that awaits. The climb will be
painful, but the view will be Glorious. There is
always purpose in pain, learn to be grateful
through the grief.*

*Praise is the power to persevere, and you shall
overcome. You are a mighty warrior; rise up into
the realms of My glorious presence; it is only there
where you will become undone and see what it
means to be undone. My song is written on the
tablet of your heart; it's time the notes came out.
The songs of Heaven are bursting with life and joy;
that is what I wish for you to experience in full. My*

*son, stop limiting yourself with your own analytical and crucial thinking and step into the place I have set for you beside Me.*

As I pressed deeper into the spirit and entered into the realms of Heaven immediately, I was taken to a place known as the court of men in white. As I walked into this place, I noticed the aesthetics of this room appeared to be a room encased in crystal and from every angle, you could see the entire universe. I was amazed to see the galaxies, planets, stars, and other heavenly bodies that surrounded and almost terrified me as I felt like I was standing in the middle of outer space.

A man walked towards me, and as he did, the floor made ripple patterns like a drop of water dripping into a still body of water. As he approached, I knew in my spirit this man was a saint in Heaven, known as John the Revelator. John had walked out of a doorway of light called a heavenly gate that had just appeared in the middle of the room. Through it I could see there was a river of fire flowing from the Throne of God.

John gave me a quill and a piece of parchment paper and instructed me to write down the revelations that were going to be released to me. He pulled an object out of his pocket and handed it to me. It looked much like a refrigerator magnet in the shape of a heart. John said this would draw me into deeper intimacy with the Father.

Suddenly, our surroundings shifted, and we were standing in his dwelling place upon the isle of Patmos. He showed me what Patmos looked like when he was on the Earth. I could see his prayer life. I understood his gift of intercession and the degree of solitude in the place where he wrote Revelation.

The scene shifted again, and a group of men came to join us in this heavenly room. These men became known to me as King David and the authors of the Book of Psalms. I was handed a scroll of the "Psalms, Hymns, and Spiritual Songs" the Father wanted me to write.

As the individuals who formed the cloud of witnesses exited the room, I was suddenly transported to another place that resembled a serene beach. Before me, a sailboat floated gently on calm waters, surrounded by the most vivid blue skies and pure white clouds that resembled cotton candy. The water was still and peaceful, reflecting the tranquility of the scene. On the boat, I saw my family effortlessly drifting with the current of a river. At that moment, I felt a deep assurance in my spirit that everything would be all right, for I knew the Father is good in every season and situation.

# Chapter 11
# His Nature Never Changes

Cultivating a lifestyle of intimacy with the Father is essential for living according to His design, from the moment we are born. Sadly, too often, the Body of Christ trades this intimate walk for a "keeping up with the Joneses" mentality. When we shift our focus away from Him, we lose sight of His goodness and His desires for our lives. It's all too easy to become caught up in doing things for God while neglecting to truly have God at the center of our actions. Before we realize it, we may find ourselves in a dry, fruitless place, longing for His presence—just as David did after his sin with Bathsheba in 2 Samuel 11. Yet, the Father is always ready to forgive, always eager to wrap His arms around us. His nature never changes, and His love for us remains steadfast, no matter where we find ourselves.

One day, with a heavy heart, I sat before the Father, weeping and seeking restoration. I felt wounded, as though I had failed to live up to His grace. I was deep in a transitional season, where it seemed like every part of my life was out of alignment. I had recently stepped down from a leadership role, following a word and promise that our assignment there was complete. But in the aftermath, our family was unexpectedly shown the door, feeling the sting of rejection. I couldn't pray or worship; all I could do was weep, convinced that I had misheard His voice and led my family astray into the wilderness. During this time, I became all too skilled at condemning myself. Yet, in the midst of my brokenness, the Father's love remained unwavering. Then, in a powerful moment, He showed up in my room, offering words of loving encouragement. He was intent on helping me release my fallen nature and embrace the fullness of my true identity.

Father said:

> *My son, be upright and of good cheer; be one who is lost in My love and not one wandering far from it. Allow yourself time to refresh and seek first My Kingdom. My presence has the joy and stability you need. It will be given freely through the flow of My spirit to your spirit within you.*

> *My son, you are so blessed and favored; do not for a second, let anything in the natural realm hold you back from your destiny. Do not listen to the lies of the adversary. Getting caught up in fallacy will ensnare you and throw you off course. Look to the heavens, for that is where your help comes from. Look to Me when you are weary, and I will give you rest. Press into the rivers of My unfailing*

*love, and I will refresh you. I will restore you, and I will carry you to the greater glory that you were destined for. Serve mightily and serve well with joy and compassion in all things. Let your heart be merciful to all those that you meet, and let love be your ultimate motivation.*

Then the Holy Spirit spoke, saying:

*What the Father has for you is amazing; Be still and stand firm. Do not rush the process. The Father is ushering in a new season. The chaff before the wind is burning, it is being blown away. The old books are being dusted off and opened, for the time is at hand for the next move of God. Mountains will be brought low, fruitless trees hacked down; dry rivers will flow anew as the day of the Lord approaches.*

*Let none be swept up in the weariness of waiting or be hindered by distraction. Great is the Father's love, and worthy are those who hold on tight to the fullness of the gifts given. Allow the rivers of the Father's love to flow through you today. The world is trying to glean from its old ways and dress them up as something new. The new thing the Father does is always fresh and innovative. Don't fall for yesterday's chaff.*

*Beautiful child of God, it is time to rise up to believe in yourself and use the gifts the Father set apart for you for His glory. It is no longer time to hide in a cave, a pew, or your home. It's time to step out, spread your wings and fly. Do not be afraid of failure but allow the effortless grace of the Father to run through you and flow through you. There's room for you to learn by error, there's room for you to try with uncertain outcomes, and there is room for you to use these grace gifts the Father has given you especially that of prophecy, to glorify His name. Build up His church. Do what He has called you to do. This season is the season of your rising up; it's time to shine like a star you are.*

As I heard this, I was taken into another vision in which I saw a pink Lily blossoming, opening, spreading out and then the petals falling off. Holy Spirit was showing me the life cycles of seasons on Earth from birth through death. As Ecclesiastes 3 speaks of life cycles, I was in a cycle of renewal, repair, and restoration.

Then, I asked the Father what He thinks about life upon the Earth. He said to me that it is special, the center of His universe and the place of His choosing for the dwelling of His children.

He said to me:

*You are a risen son by the resurrection power of Christ. Walk confidently in knowing I am with you in and through all things. I don't want you to toil and spin; do not worry about where you will be or what tomorrow brings. Take charge today and serve wholeheartedly in all things, no matter how menial they seem, for I will go forth before you to prepare the place you belong in. You will go to a place of My choosing, a place where you and your flock will flourish and grow. Let your heart be still and unafraid of uncertainty. I will never leave you or fail you; be still and know that I am God.*

## Stepping into Breakthrough

In another engagement with Heaven, I was told:

*Today will be a day of glistening, shimmering, and sparkling in My Kingdom. You are like a diamond in the rough, being shaped, cut, and pressed to become the beautiful jewel you are destined to be.*

(I saw an image of a child in a basket like Moses in the basket floating down a river).

*Child, you are being sheltered in the Father's arms and riding on the flowing river of His love, He will hold you tight, and even when you lose your grip, you will not stumble or fall but be snug and secure in His loving arms. Pain is never part of His processes; growth is.*

*You will start a church one day; it will be different than those that came before, and it will be My home and My dwelling place of My presence... many will come from far and wide to seek God. Their lives will be transformed, marriages will be healed, addictions broken, the strong tower of the Lord shall be the supreme resting place for those who love God and are called according to His purposes.*

In the spirit I saw magnolia trees with white fuzzy buds on them—I saw rainbow whirlwinds and cascading rainbows all around. He continued speaking:

*My child, be still knowing that there is such an amazing breakthrough that is coming. It's on its way and finally manifesting here. This conference that you're going to attend next week will be fabulous; it will be miraculous, it will be amazing. Such wonder and awe will strike all who are there as they see that which I will do in their midst, even in the midst of you and your wife; such a newness of life, such a breakthrough, as you have never imagined, will be coming from it.*

*The enemy has seen the expectation in your heart; when you have expectation in your heart, the light of your glow changes, it becomes brighter, it becomes bolder, it becomes more resilient to the frequencies of the Earth! This change is noticeable by the powers of Heaven and also the kingdom of darkness; when the kingdom of darkness notices such a change in a believer's shine, they try to snuff it out. They try to throw wet blankets over the fire; they try to sow seeds of doubt, seeds of trepidation, and seeds of fear, and make them forget about the thing which they are hoping on, and believing in, and trusting that it will be done.*

*My child, see that your heart is guarded against such things; this is where meditating upon the Word is a vital warfare tactic; when a believer reads the Scriptures and knows the Word, the Word takes root in their heart, and that root deepens the more that they read it, the more that they eat of it; it strengthens their spirit, but it also strengthens the root. That route bears fruit upwards, that fruit becomes faith, that fruit becomes hope, that fruit becomes joy, that fruit becomes a reminder to the believer knowing that they are a child of God, that they are a son or a daughter and that there is nothing and no one that could take the promises of God away from them.*

*Look at the instances that have taken place in the past weeks of your life, the moments where you have been overflowing with joy and faith. Have you felt different? Have you had more pep in your step? Have you had more of an expectation of the miraculous?*

*Now, take into consideration the times where there has been worrying your life. Did you feel like praying in those moments? Did you feel like encouraging and extorting others? As your mind focuses on rising up and overcoming, the key to the seasons, the ebbs and flows, the battles between soul and spirit, and the will of the flesh is to be rooted and grounded in the Word of God. It is a sure foundation.*

# Chapter 12
# Uprooted and Replanted

On the morning of February 5th, 2022, I sat in deep prayer, processing one of the biggest decisions of my life with the Lord. Just days earlier, my wife and I had traveled to Fort Myers, Florida, for a conference. We anticipated a peaceful time away, without our children, simply enjoying the presence of God. But God had different plans. In His infinite wisdom, the next 72 hours became a whirlwind of mystical experiences—filled with signs, wonders, visions, and encounters. What we didn't realize at the time was that these moments were baby steps on a path toward God's promises, a path that would change the course of our lives and the lives of our children.

During this time, we had been praying about moving out of New York. The spiritual climate of our home state no longer seemed conducive to the life we wanted to build for our children. We wanted to be sure we were hearing the Father's heart clearly, so we had been fasting and praying for guidance. While we initially felt drawn to Tennessee or the

Carolinas, the Father had a different plan. Upon arriving in Florida, the Lord began speaking clearly to both of us. But for me, He asked something specific: *"Are you willing to put EVERYTHING on the altar, trust Me, and move here, not knowing if you will have a house or a job?"* I said yes, even though my wife and I had never envisioned relocating to Florida. We knew, however, that we had no choice but to trust God and embrace His plan.

We returned home, listed our house for sale, and began the process of obediently stepping into this new journey, trusting that God's best awaited us.

## A Divine Word

As I sat before the Lord, He spoke the following to me:

*The road before you is long, narrow, and winding, but the destination is beautiful. It is glory-filled and resonates with the frequencies of the heavenly realm. It has paths paved with gold and mountains of silver. Let knowledge, wisdom, and understanding guide you.*

*You have stepped into a new chapter. Together with your wife, in this ministry, and with new friends, you will encounter divine connections and destinations not yet seen. Trust My promptings, obey My voice, listen to My instruction, and watch for the signs. You asked for more, and in kindness, I will show you many. Those around you see what I see, and the time is now for you to behold your own heart and the way I crafted you. I see the delicacy in how you speak and act; I know your heart's intent and true desire. I have tested it to ensure it is not faulty in its desire to serve Me wholeheartedly.*

*Battles and storms will come, but I will establish you on a rock foundation and shelter you through them. Prepare to be blissfully supported as what I am bringing into the natural realm manifests before your eyes. You will see, My child. You will feel My presence. You will see in the spirit and the natural realm what I have called you to. Fret not. Be still and know. The time is at hand for advancement into a new season. The door of destiny is opening—stay the course!*

As I diligently wrote every word, Heaven continued to speak and said:

*Sometimes, you must leave where you are comfortable and step onto the mission field, but you will be connected in the ways I want you to be. If you ask, I will order your steps to make things easy. The heart can be deceiving, but My will for you is secured in My love for you.*

*Your wife and children will be happiest and thriving in the south (meaning Florida). I want you to have prophetic mothering and fathering. It's time to step into the fullness of your destiny and calling, There will be many invited. You are to go, for what I have for you is extraordinary, but there is much to be done between now and then. Don't miss a moment of it by pondering and sulking - wondering if you heard accurately. Instead, just believe that all things will be revealed and trust the process. This isn't warfare. It's preparation! Women in labor travail with labor pains, and so do the prophets, evangelists, apostles, and leaders who are in the gestation period of what is being birthed within them.*

In another engagement the same week, Heaven continued to speak about the things we were going to endure and grow through in this transitional period. I felt like Shadrach, Meshach, and Abednego must have during their era. It seemed like all hell was breaking loose in my life, and the fire had been turned up seven times hotter than ever before. As I sat seeking the Father these were His words to encourage me.

*My son, you are adored and loved beyond all your wildest dreams. At times, it seems you may walk through hardships even in your relationship, but all things work for My purposes. All things lost are being (and have been) restored.*

*The adversary hates to see the children of God glimmer with glee and celebrate with joy, thanksgiving, and praise. He goes after immature sons to pull them from the righteous path and tempts mature sons to see if they will falter in their surefooted ways. Be keen to his loathsome plots. One who walks in My ways and follows My path will never lose footing and stumble from My mountaintop.*

*Behold, I am doing a new thing: be aware of your surroundings in the natural and supernatural realm and be alerted to The Light's advance and the retreat of wickedness. You are called as one who will rip down strongholds that ensnare those I have called by My name.*

*You are anointed to uproot, to plant, to cut down and to build up, engage wisdom and understanding for the complete magnitude of what you are stepping into. There is abundant grace in this prophetic call. Do not be deceived or detoured by the fleshly cravings for what I have not yet released you into. Trust My timing and My planning, there will be many opportunities along the way to operate in fullness and growth of your calling. They will be exciting and invigorating to your spirit. This is a formative place, a ground of preparation and growth. A place to learn and prepare for that which is yet to come and is coming soon. Trust is putting your whole trust and faith in Me. It's knowing My promises are concrete, steadfast, and immovable. The promises of God can never be shaken or taken from those who I have promised.*

As this engagement concluded, I heard the Holy Spirit say, *"Heaven is steamrolling the enemy!!"*

I began worshipping, and in a vision, I saw Jesus walk across a field before me with the disciples. I saw myself as a young boy running up to him, He placed a crown on my head and a golden mantle on my shoulders. As I continued to worship, I heard the Father telling me that He was well pleased. I asked Father about the songs of deliverance He sings over me at night and I heard Him singing about demolishing the witchcraft, scattering His arrows against My foes, and scattering the enemy's camps. This brought forth great peace as, at this moment, I had a desperate need for it.

## Following The Lord's Command

As I continued to wrestle with the prospect of leaving our families, all that we loved and our support system in New York, I stayed vigilant, spending time with the Lord, praying for confirmation and journaling all that was said. I was taken into a vision where I saw my angels pouring a bucket of living water over me and then walking with Jesus through fields of wheat. I was reminded of Colossians 3:1 that describes being seated (spiritually) in heavenly places, and realized from Heaven's perspective my spirit was continually in Heaven when He said to me, *"You never left."* As I heard the words, a rainbow appeared in the sky.

I was reminded of words Father spoke when I was in the shower, telling me to connect with an amazing woman of God who would later become our Pastor and Real Estate Agent, Aprile Osborne. The Lord showed me that there was a spiritual mothering of sorts and a cause for Joelene and me to connect with the church she pastored, Safe House church. I was reminded by Heaven of a mandate, calling, and prophetic words spoken over the congregants days before the conference. The Lord showed me this was a place that was called to heal the lost, broken, and drug-addicted, as well as to care for the orphans. These things were near to my heart and calling as well.

Suddenly, the scene shifted. Jesus and I were before the throne. The Father spoke and said:

> *My son, today will be a day like no other. Come expecting the unexpected; no eye has seen, nor ear has heard what I will do in thy midst; you will see the abominations of men's minds and hearts crumble, and in their place shall remain the cross*

*of Christ and throne of the Most High. The new*
*wine has been poured out, and the game is on to*
*see who will be able to stand in the presence of the*
*Lord.*

I cried to the Father and prayed and asked for deeper intimacy and encounters for myself and my wife. As I did, He reminded me of the yellow scarf of grace and plush white robe He had given me in an earlier vision. Father said it was the robe of messiah's comfort, to comfort the sorrow and anguish that comes to those whose hearts cry out with passion in intercession for His people.

I said, "I give you all my self-awareness and concern of judgment of others."

And Father simply said:

*It doesn't matter. Be free in loving Me, be free*
*to be who I made you to be. Don't worry for your*
*wife or your family; let them have their own*
*experience. I have built you differently. I have*
*equipped you to transcend beyond a religious*
*experience, you have been given the keys of Elijah,*
*the access of Moses, the intimacy of Abraham and*
*the mantle of Elisha. You have been given the*
*heart and tears of Jeremiah and are of His*
*namesake. Rise up and come out of the hidden*
*place. This is your season. Let Me bear the burden*

*of your yoke, and you enjoy the blessing of My presence and nearness.*

As I sought His word to comfort the aches of my soul, the Holy Spirit brought me to the following scriptures to further confirm His promises.

*The seacoast shall be pastures, with shelters for shepherds and folds for flocks. The coast shall be for the remnant of the house of Judah; they shall feed their flocks there; in the houses of Ashkelon, they shall lie down at evening. For the Lord their God will intervene for them and return their captives. (Zephaniah 2:6-7)*

## Prophecy, Prayer, Faith, and Trust

In a subsequent engagement, as I waited upon the Lord in the Secret Place He spoke to my heart and said:

*My son, the time has come for an uprising in the north and an uprising in the south, and the east wind will bring the inclusion of territories east and west into the fray that will dismantle the former things as you have known them. But fret not as this trouble comes upon the Earth. Shift your focus to My throne of Grace, and no trouble of the Earth shall betray your mind and such you into frequencies of worry and fear.*

The encouragement was timely as I was amid the natural changes in my life, and in the media and on the news were wars and rumors of wars. The thoughts and opinions of man fed into these fears with prognostications of the times and seasons before us and the happenings in the Middle East. As I sought the Lord's direction to calm my angst, He spoke truth to my spirit to help me separate myself from these prognostications and enter back into His truth.

Father said:

> *The time has not yet come for the war in Har Megiddo, but the times and seasons of your realm are rapidly shifting in that direction; the enemy seeks to be bolder and more blatant in his thieving and immoral activities, and many have had their hearts grow cold to sin. Many have turned back from repentance and embraced the immorality, yet even more are waking up to their destiny as sons. There is no more black and white, slave and free, sinner and saint, but as you have come to realize higher degrees of the Knowledge of Father's Kingdom and the hunger to walk these paths with the King. As you have spoken it, it's no longer a time to sit in a building in a seat. It is time to rise up as sons, take hold of your heavenly inheritance and walk it out upon the Earth.*

The Holy Spirit said:

*In Matthew, Jesus walks up to a fig tree and authoritatively commands it to shrivel up and bear no fruit, and it obeys. This is your inheritance because We (Father, Son, and Holy Spirit) are one in you. It is your destiny and your inheritance to command darkness to shrivel up and bear no fruit. Your words have the power to battle back that which has deceived many into believing it had power. Its only power is fear and lies against which you stand mightily radiating the light of the Father's Glory in Christ Jesus.*

As this encounter ended, the Holy Spirit brought me into the scripture He had referenced:

*Now, early in the morning, as He was returning to the city, He became hungry. Seeing a lone fig tree by the road, He came up to it and found nothing on it except leaves only. And He said to it, 'May no fruit ever come from you again!' And the fig tree shriveled up at once. When the disciples saw it, they were astonished.*

*'How did the fig tree shrivel on the spot?' they asked.*

*Yeshua answered them, 'Amen, I tell you, if you have faith and do not doubt, not only will you do what was done to the fig tree, but even if you say to this mountain, "Be taken up and thrown into the sea," it will happen. And whatever you ask in prayer, trusting, you shall receive.' (Matthew 21:18-22, TLV)*

125

# Chapter 13

# Living on the Altar of the Lord

As my journey into the deeper things of God continued and the days progressed toward the new territory the Lord was bringing us to dwell in, I started learning about the cost of intimacy with God.

It's possible to fellowship with other believers and talk about God without ever truly learning how to spend time alone with Him. I was beginning to understand that as someone who deeply hungered and thirsted for more of God, there was a cost to pursuing Him. It wasn't just a price to pay—it was a process of dying to myself. I had to consistently deny my flesh and surrender fully to the leading of the Holy Spirit. To me, this became known as a process of living on the altar in which I would surrender myself daily to the Father's will. I had to surrender because the emotional strain and stress of selling a house, moving, and relocating our entire family felt overwhelming, like a heavy burden to bear.

One morning, as I waited on the Lord in prayer, I was drawn into a vision where I walked side by side with the Lord through a picturesque meadow in Heaven. As we continued, it felt as though I was standing under a rain cloud in the midst of a gentle spring shower. Each drop that fell carried the essence of the Father, enveloping me in an overwhelming sense of love. As the heavenly sun shower bathed me, I looked up to see rainbows arching overhead. The living waters continued to pour down, and deep within, I knew I was being showered with the Father's abundant goodness. As I looked ahead, I noticed angels gathered around with shofars blowing them throughout the heavens and at each blast, there was a resonating frequency of deliverance. In this moment deliverance was definitely needed from the overwhelming thoughts that had been at the top of my mind. Coming out of the vision, the Holy Spirit led me into the Word first with an encouragement to speak life over my situations and then to exhort me with the Father's love.

*Thou shalt also decree a thing, and it shall be established unto thee: And the light shall shine upon thy ways. (Job 22:28, KJV)*

*For He enjoys His faithful lovers. He adorns the humble with His beauty, and He loves to give them victory. His godly lovers triumph in the glory of God, and their joyful praises will rise even while others sleep. God's high and holy praises fill their mouths, for their shouted praises are their weapons of war! These warring weapons will bring vengeance on the nations and every resistant power—to bind kings with chains and rulers with iron shackles. Praise-filled warriors will enforce the judgment decreed against their enemies. This is the honor He gives to all His godly lovers. Hallelujah! Praise the Lord. (Psalms 149:4-9, TPT)*

As I meditated upon these words, Father spoke to me and said:

*I am bringing you and your family out of Babylon, My son. I didn't fail Moses, and I won't fail you. The time will be coming for you to move out into the fullness of what I have called you and your family to do, but for now, I want you to be a student again.*

As the Father said, this I was stunned. In my mind the reason He was moving us was to help build a community and to pour out what had been sewn into us, but here He was correcting me and telling me I was to become a student again.

Father could see the look of confusion on my face, and He continued to speak, saying:

*You will grow and be stretched in ways that perfectly align with your journey. This is a season of shedding incorrect teachings you once accepted and embracing truths you've never encountered before—truths discovered by those who relentlessly sought Me with unwavering determination, no matter the obstacles. You will be taught by those who followed My voice despite all the trials and who walked by My side through fire and flood.*

I knew He was referring to the leaders and mentors He was bringing us to in the new land.

Father warned me and said:

*You will want to quit. You will want to turn back and give up at times, but these are just outdated mindsets that need to be left behind. When you push through, what awaits you will be beyond anything you can imagine. I am with you every step of the way—I will never leave or forsake you. You don't need to seek validation for your gifts or from your gifts. You are in a secure and safe place to learn how to operate in them fully. Don't let the constraints of religion rob you of the treasures I have for you.*

# Season to Launch

In a subsequent encounter, I saw an eagle screeching across the sky in the spirit, and I heard Heaven say, *"This is your season to launch."*

As I looked around at the scenery to see what else Heaven had to say, I noticed that I was in the Throne Room. I could see the Sea of Glass like crystal beneath my feet depicted in Revelation 4.

As I marveled at the beauty of the Throne Room, the Lord began to minister to me about the various realms and dimensions of Heaven. He explained that we were in the Third Heaven, but at the current time, I could not venture to the higher levels of Heaven.

The Father began to explain to me that the realms He was referring to are places or destinations. He explained:

> *As humans have three realms between our soul, body, and spirit, the Father, Jesus, and Holy Spirit also can be likened to three separate realms within Heaven.*

I was thoroughly confused and, at the same time, enthralled to learn more. The Father explained:

*The Earth is a realm, as the Kingdom of Heaven
is a realm, and all of these realms can be traveled
to or visited in the spirit.*

I started to understand that the Father was helping my soul to understand that although we would be absent in the body from our spiritual family and friends we were leaving behind in New York, we were present in the spirit in Heaven. As the Father continued to speak, I started to see visions of our departure from the place we were in and our transition to the place He was leading us to.

As I watched this eagerly, I could feel the joy, excitement, and bittersweet sadness of leaving those we love to venture toward His calling for us. Father looked at me lovingly as my eyes welled up with tears and said the time was soon to come. I nodded as if to say, "I know."

Holy Spirit sweetly comforted me and whispered:

*This season is a season of expanding, stretching,
and growing. There is an increase coming and with
it a mantle of greater authority in the prophetic,
your ministry, your calling, your family, your work
life and in your ministry with the Courts of
Heaven. This increase will be tenfold in measure
and propel you forward into a new phase and new
dimension upon the Earth. Continue to press into
Father's love, joy, and good pleasure to develop*

*you into one who carries His nature and character in all things.*

As I meditated upon this and felt a bit more excited about the journey ahead, Holy Spirit said:

*BREAKTHROUGH IS COMING! Advancement is coming! Ease is coming!*

Father said:

*If you would only be still and trust, you would know I will never leave you hurting or broken. I will never abandon you. I hear your heart's cries and I've seen the brutality against you, I've seen the fire of your intercession rising up and burning up the yokes of heaviness.*

*Rise up, push back, press on. Victory is yours because you are mine; if others trade with you unjustly, do not curse them to die, for they are dead in their sin; be not dead in yours; you are an ambassador of My Kingdom.*

*This is what new levels feel like: crushing, pressing, fire and pain, but in the end, you can trust in My name. I am your deliverance; when you call, I will answer, My heart cries when others don't listen to My voice, as it does when you don't listen to it.*

I felt bashful as I had been spending a lot of time getting emotional and admittedly had not been listening to His voice repeatedly telling me to be still.

Father continued to speak to me as I sat hanging on every word:

*This move will build you up; all things work for My purpose and My glory. Both you and your wife are being transformed.*

*Remember the vision and word I gave you about intercession?*

As I thought back, I recalled how Heaven often would use movies or television and things from my childhood to build out visions. In this instance, the Father was referring to a memory of a childhood past time cartoon called *Dragon Ball Z*. In this cartoon, whenever the protagonist, a martial artist named Goku, was up against the ropes and his family and home under siege, he turned his emotion into a powerup, if you will, which gave Him enhanced skill, speed, and agility.

The Father brought to mind some hard conversations with loved ones we had just walked through, where others lashed out at our family with news of our moving. Leaving us feeling alone and rejected. The Father said:

*Last night, when you were up against the ropes, feeling beaten and defeated and feeling the weight of your family's hurt and distress, a fire was lit. This was an ethereal and eternal blast of dynamite that went off in your spirit and the fire of God erupted from within in prayer.*

He put His hand on my shoulder, looking at me like a proud Papa, and said:

*From this day forth, you will walk in that fire and steward that fire to intercede for the needs of those you love and those who need a prayer warrior to rise up and push back the darkness. The fire is within you! When things are at their bleakest, dig deep in prayer and transform into the fiery intercessor I created you to be. You are a dread champion; you are a victor over darkness because My spirit is in you. Push back, punch back and press on!*

Holy Spirit said:

*The darkness has been lifted from you. Now you are a child of the light; go forth into newness and let your light shine.*

*Many are the paths of the wicked, but only the path of righteousness leads to the Lord's blessings. Do not stumble where foolishness entices and seeks to derail you; allow wisdom a seat at your gate. Invite her daily. Let counsel, knowledge and understanding accompany her, and this heavenly entourage will lead you on all My paths that are peace. Your light will shine as noonday, and you will lead many to prosper in the land of the living by the hand of the Lord if you will heed My cries and allow My Spirit to guide you always.*

Father concluded and said,

*This is a season of upheaval; moving is an upheaval. Do not allow the upheaval to distract your heart and mind. Walk firmly, rooted, and grounded in the peace of God that transcends understanding. Walk firmly rooted and grounded in the Word of God. Be still; in stillness and quiet you will experience My rest. Be patient, Pursue boldness in the faith and in the things of God. Do not let current events shift your perspective or focus.*

*The responsibility you have in the natural does not have to overpower your spiritual prowess. Keep your mind focused on the throne above, not the Earth below. The King of kings is your shield and body armor, so run swiftly into His arms and lean not on your own understanding. This is your time of preparation, My beloved son.*

As I looked onward into Heaven, pondering all that had been said, I saw a gold valley filled with cottages. I stood atop a cliff overlooking the streets of gold and houses of chrysoprase.[8] I noticed there was a field of deer, lions, and wild things behind me, coexisting peacefully. I could see peace on the horizon that could be felt in the form of a large bay with boats sailing across it. Above me in the sky were three radiant rainbows and many birds flying and singing praises to God.

As this engagement ended, Heaven simply said:

*This is a new season and a new journey for you.*

---

[8] Chrysoprase is a semi-precious gemstone that ranges from light to intense green.

# Chapter 14

# Into the Unknown

On the morning of June 21, 2022, as I stepped into Heaven, I felt a mix of nervousness and excitement. This was the day I was to depart for "the promised land." I gathered my belongings, my dog and one of the kids and embarked on the journey. I had a long drive ahead of me and resolved to go ahead of my wife and the rest of the kids in order to close on our new home and put things in order ahead of their arrival. We left at about 3 a.m. to drive to Florida, tearfully waving goodbye to our former home state of New York. I knew great things awaited as we were destined for the place the Lord had called us to.

As I drove down the highway, in the spirit, I saw all of Heaven celebrating and applauding us. I heard the Father saying, *"Well done, My good and faithful servant, well done."*

I was moved to tears as I witnessed Heaven's encouragement for the assignments that my wife and I were engaged in. This act of obedience was painful to our flesh, but Heaven's encouragement was needed and welcome. Heaven said:

*You have completed the Father's good work in this chapter of your journey and have accomplished all that He desired you to accomplish in New York.*

As I continued to drive, I inquired of the Lord to know the prayer needs for the trip ahead and the burdens of the Father's heart. I was taken into a place called the Court of Records and shown a folder in the Courts of Heaven called the Outstanding Folder.

Inside the folder were several items I needed to address through intercessory prayer. As I opened the folder in the spirit, one item immediately stood out. It was an extravagantly wrapped gift box that seemed to beckon me to open it. Inside, I discovered a new tiara and crown for both me and my wife. Alongside them were wedding rings, intricately bound together, symbolizing not only our union but also our union with Jesus as the third cord in our marriage. This divine connection strengthened our bond, as we had given Him permission to rule and reign over our marital union.

Next, I noticed a key ring in the folder, holding five keys that dangled from it. Curious, I inquired of the Holy Spirit what these keys were for. As soon as I asked the question, five doors suddenly appeared before me, each corresponding to a key on the ring. By faith, I began unlocking and opening each door.

Behind the first door was a revelation of new ministries and leadership roles that awaited not just me and my wife but also our children. These new opportunities were ways we would serve the Lord in this next season of our lives.

The second door opened to a breathtaking landscape of golden hills, a shimmering golden sky, and fields of golden flowers. Everything behind the door radiated with pure gold, stretching into eternity. I discerned that this vision symbolized our inheritance as sons and daughters of God— a glimpse of the promises and rewards He had stored up for us. Heaven confirmed and spoke:

> *This is payback for what has been lost, what has been stolen, and the harvest you will reap from all that you have sown.*

Behind the third door, I saw trumpeting angels blowing shofars. Their powerful sounds resonated throughout creation, delivering and purifying everything in their reach. I understood that these frequencies were also preparing new realms for us to occupy, setting the stage for our arrival. This vision reaffirmed the Father's promise to go before us and prepare a place for us.

Behind the fourth door, I saw a burst of vibrant, colorful musical notes and scales dancing in the air. Heaven spoke,

*"These are the rhythms and cadences of Heaven, flowing upon the Earth."* Beyond the frequencies, I saw angels worshipping with joy and many musical instruments of heavenly design. Heaven declared:

> *These angels are now being assigned to your lives for the next season. You are to grow in prophetic worship, singing, and playing instruments for the glory of God. His angels will assist you in writing songs from Heaven and learning to play from Heaven.*

As this revelation unfolded, I gained a deeper understanding: this was not just about music but an equipping for our family and future generations to carry the destiny the Lord had designed for us. Heaven explained that the angels would help us fulfill these callings, enabling us to glorify God with creative worship straight from the heart of Heaven. With this promise, I felt a stirring of joy in my spirit. Heaven spoke that the angels would assist with the callings upon our lives, that our hearts were to be filled with merriment and worship of the Lord.

Finally, it was time to open door number five. As my hand turned the key, I heard in the spirit: *"This is the great door."* With anticipation, I stepped forward, and the moment the door swung open, ripples of silver light began to dance around me. Above, a radiant Glory cloud of silver hovered, filling the atmosphere with a holy stillness. From the door flowed a stream of silver water, glimmering with life and motion.

Heaven declared:

*This is the color of Grace, the Father's grace for His children. This is the grace for one to move into a new season, the grace for you to be replanted, to flourish, to comfort one another, in grace and unity together as the Father has intended since the beginning of time.*

I was also told that this grace was the embodiment and the origin of the euphemisms that say, *"Every cloud has a silver lining."* Heaven revealed that the silver linings we experience in life are manifestations of the Father's grace and goodness, offered for all His children to enjoy.

## Getting Comfortable Being Uncomfortable

During seasons when the Lord moves to bless us, there is often an intense period of crushing and pruning that must take place. These times can leave one feeling discouraged, disinterested, or as though they are floundering without purpose. Transition often resembles a wilderness experience. Yet, just as Jesus emerged from His forty days in the wilderness empowered by the Holy Spirit, our own transitions and wildernesses can be used by God to propel us forward.

As I continued to engage with Heaven and sought the Father's heart for comfort, I learned a profound lesson: we must embrace the uncomfortable places to allow Him to complete His perfect work in us.

One morning, as I sat alone with the Father in our new home, my soul was in turmoil—utterly resistant to the idea of starting anew. I felt like a stranger in a foreign land, carrying not only my own grief but also that of my family, who were also feeling lost and unsettled. As I turned my ear to hear from Heaven, the Father comforted me with these words:

> *This will be a season that will be written on the tapestry of your heart, and it will define who you are, My child. If you seek My ways and My face, who you become will be like that beautiful butterfly that spent a season in a cocoon.*

> *The pride has been humbled out of you; all of My children can be prideful at times, but your story is unique. Do not view the testimony of another brother or sister as fitting every place you are growing into. Do not check every box of their test, trial, and tribulation as if you are to walk the same path; you are not. You are to learn the encouragement and the lessons they learned so that you may pass your own tests and advance past your current state. Do not be caught in a state*

*of stagnation or procrastination, be caught up in*
*My love.*

As the Father spoke these words of encouragement and correction to me, I noticed a heavenly gate opened, and some men in white linen walked through. These men were Daniel and Joseph. They approached and spoke to me, saying, "Do not fear the long-suffering of a long season, for the process of purification is timely yet rewarding." Father agreed and said:

> *Today, I just want you to be emotionally still,*
> *for in stillness and quiet, you will find My voice.*
> *Seek first the Kingdom of God; not everything is*
> *about pain and growth but the place of*
> *brokenness, which allows you to hear My voice*
> *clearer than ever before.*

I knew they were encouraging me not to strive but to settle into our new surroundings. My heart longed to immediately be plugged back into a community thriving and serving as we had for so long before the move, yet in the spirit, it was as if we were a plant that had been uprooted and repotted elsewhere. I knew we needed time for our roots to grow and settle into the new foundation in which we had been placed.

I was taken into a vision in which I was walking in a garden with Father. As we walked, He spoke to me and said:

*My child, you don't need to earn your stripes; remember you were bought with a price; you were chosen. I want you to rest in this season. Rest in Me, rest in My presence and let your countenance, your ambition, and your passion be restored. Let the busyness that has overtaken you become ease and peace; don't allow the business of warfare the enemy had put before you consume your time. Don't let it distract you from Me. How will your lamp get filled with oil if you are too busy to go and be poured into?*

I looked at His adoring eyes as He pleaded with me to understand His heart. He continued:

*For how you have honored My chosen and anointed ones I am well pleased. For how you have honored others, I will honor you in My Kingdom.*

As He spoke, I took notice of a table that had appeared and upon it was a giant sheet cake with an uncountable number of candles. I asked, "Why the cake?"

He responded:

*We are celebrating you today, Jeremy. Today is the dawning of a new day, a new season a new step out on the path of your destiny in Christ. Today is a day in which there will be no turning back. The faucets are turned on. The floodgates are open. The chaff will be blown away, the dust removed, the gunk expunged, and every hindrance destroyed so that you may move ahead into the next dimension of your calling.*

Holy Spirit spoke to me and said:

*You are completely free from the past and unhindered to do the Father's will.*

An angel appeared before me, holding a small object that resembled a miniature "wheel within a wheel," like the one described in Ezekiel.

Heaven said:

*This is a watcher; it is assigned to watch over the new territories you are being given authority and jurisdiction over. Do not underestimate its significance due to its size, for its size symbolizes the infancy stage of this new territory and calling upon your life. There is much to be birthed in your life over the next twenty years. Consider this a sign and a wonder—a token of the trials and tests of these formative years.*

*These are years of teething, years where you are to learn vital and developmental Kingdom truths. These revelations will shape you into who you are meant to become. Lean not on your gifting but upon the Giver of gifts. Do not wonder why things may not seem to flow freely; instead, seek first the Kingdom of God and the Father's heart. From Him will flow the torrents of refreshment and revelation—streams of wisdom and grace that will pour out in an unstoppable and immeasurable measure.*

As the words resonated in my spirit, I heard a voice declaring, *"You have no lack, dear one."*

The voice repeated with emphasis, "**YOU HAVE NO LACK, DEAR ONE!**"

As I heard these words spoken, I became aware that Jesus had joined us and was the one speaking. As He spoke, the frequencies of these words shook me to my core like the magnitude of an earthquake, yet it was a lion's roar. I could see crusty, dry places shattering and breaking off me. These dry places looked like pieces of a statue that had broken off, and underneath, fresh new skin was peering through. I heard the Lord say, *"You are indeed a new wine skin, now be filled with new wine."*

The Father then spoke my heart. You see, as this encounter was taking place, something inside me desired to run to the phone and call a prophet friend of mine to seek a confirming work of direction. Yet, in this hour the Father was teaching me only to hear and listen to His voice to receive prophetic words for the course of my life directly from Him.

He spoke to me, and my heart began to burn as I heard these words:

*Do you need a word? Here is My word to you. Be filled with sweet new wine; let your drink become the wine of joy and gladness in your belly. As you worship, you will become drunk in the Spirit with My love which is from everlasting to everlasting.*

As this encounter ended, I felt forced to my knees and then fell headlong, laying prostrate on the floor. All I could do was weep, repent of my wrong heart posture and praise His goodness. The Father is close to those with a broken spirit and contrite heart, yet the choice to let Him in to comfort and heal is ours to make.

# Chapter 15

# The Process

As I engaged Heaven one September morning, the Holy Spirit began showing me my later years and the places I would be called to travel. I started to see visions of cherry blossoms and architecture reminiscent of what one might expect to see in Japan. I also noticed many territorial spirits, but the Holy Spirit informed me that this was because the area needed ministry. As the scene faded, I heard the Father speaking to me, revealing things that were to take place in the present. He said:

> *My son, the events that you are living through right now are part of a preparation process; lean into it. Allow the fat to be trimmed away and burnt off. Let the chaff be blown off of your heart and posture its song to be a worship offering. Abandon the worldly desires and seek Me fully. I will never disappoint or abandon you; I will never beat, forsake, or shame you. Release your burdens unto Me, and I will give you rest. Your soul cannot*

*fathom the things your spirit yearns for, the peace and refreshing that comes with knowing Me fully.*

Father continued,

*I want to tell you that you are doing a fine job. There will be tests and trials ahead of you. Some you will pass, some you may fail. I want you to know it's not a system of pass or fail. These instances present a chance to grow and learn, to be pruned and to bear fruit. You are a seed to be planted in the rich soil of My Word, and you will never go astray on a path of unrighteousness.*

*Allow your spirit to gorge itself on the fruit of the Word, for the Word of God is the vitamin your spirit needs to thrive. Indulge yourself on My innermost thoughts and find Me in the secret place. These are the keys to survival and the keys to success. Ask, Seek, Find.[9]*

In another engagement, the Father gave me the following exhortation:

*Do not buckle under the pressure, My beloved son. Stand tall, stand tall, Man of God! You are more than a son; you are a King. In the pressure, coal is pressed and refined, making the most*

---

[9] Matthew 7:7, NIV

*beautiful diamonds. I am making things fall together. I am collapsing what is not meant for you.*

*Allow Me to do away with all that is unnecessary, and allow yourself to embrace this cultivation of minerals, resources, and the heavenly beauty that is being made in this season. Remember the olive tree and its fruit. Olives are beaten to get oil; grapes are trodden upon to make new wine. Slaves and servants that may have been beaten are not broken of their spirit but strengthened of My spirit. Let My love have its perfect work even in this hour. Travail until you prevail; press in to press on; don't fall away. Fall into My arms. I am with you always, dear one!!! RISE UP, RISE UP, RISE UP MAN OF GOD!*

As my Heavenly Father encouraged me, tears streamed down my face. I felt lost, homesick, and starving for community in our new home. In this new territory, I felt very insecure. I began to question if I had indeed heard from the Father accurately or if I had missed it. As these soulish thoughts tried to invade my mind, the Father's voice rang through, and He continued to speak:

*You are not the first of all My sons to have self-confidence issues. Moses, Paul, Timothy, Noah, Jeremiah, Elijah...must I go on? All these mighty men of valor shared in your trial, but know the limit is only imposed by your own mind. These meditations are of your own soul. I have set you free, but of your own will, you choose to doubt. Of your own will, you can choose rebellion or obedience. Of your own will, you may choose to open your mouth and release what I will fill it with, or you can choose to keep silent, but those who are silent at a time to voice their shofar blasts will be those caught in ruin.*

*What I have put inside you is greatness. You are yoked to Me; you are yoked to Jesus; you are no longer a man of shyness and timidity. Rise up, man of God and unleash the fire! This is the time, this is the season, this is the moment when you leave your cave of comfort. As a snail or hermit crab grows, it seeks a larger home. Similarly, to pursue your calling, you must leave your comfort zone.*

*It is time to swim out into the sea of calling. I have not chosen you to keep silent in this hour. I have given others' eyes to see the weight and value of what I have hidden within you. Now is the time to open your eyes so that you may see, hear, and behold. The time has come to step into the fullness of what you are called to do. Pray, intercede, preach, teach, evangelize, and pastor. No longer shall you be allowed to sit in a pew and decay. Your time is here to step onto the pulpit and obey*

*My voice. All of Heaven will respond as you open your mouth and herein lies the opposition.*

As I listened intently, I was truly amazed at how deeply the Father could see into My heart. I was completely unaware of why I felt so sheepish. Yet the Father knew the source of my insecurity was simply fear. As I sat prayerfully repenting of embracing fear, a final word from Father came forth, giving me a much-needed boost of confidence:

*This next season is one of magnification and glorification for My namesake. In the hour to come, you will surpass your limits. The enemy has been running scared, but no longer shall his word bind your mind. Rise up, beloved. I am proud to call you My son. Rise up and spread your wings. It's your time to shine, My precious star.*

## Assurances

As I entered Heaven on another occasion, I found myself standing in a vast meadow that was bathed in golden light. The meadow was filled with beautiful flowers of all kinds, and the air was filled with the sweet fragrance of nature. As I walked through the meadow, I saw a magnificent horse named Daphne standing in the distance. She was an angelic horse with a light radiating from her that was otherworldly.

As I approached her and patted her mane, I asked her what message Heaven had for me today. In response, she spoke with a voice that was gentle yet powerful and said, "Surety—being sure of oneself." Her words resonated deep within me, and I knew that there was more to this message.

As I listened, I heard a voice from Heaven speaking. It was a voice that was both comforting and reassuring, and it filled me with a sense of peace. The voice said that every place where I set foot is where the Father has ordained for me to go. I realized that my life was not a random sequence of events but a purposeful journey that was carefully planned by God.

The voice went on to explain that many people believe life happens by chance, and when things don't go as expected, they fall into pits of sadness, depression, and despair. However, in doing so, they miss out on the opportunities the Father has given them to touch the lives of those around them. Whether it be through being an encourager, an intercessor, an exhorter, or simply greeting someone in need with a smile, hug, or kind word, we all have the power to make a difference.

The message from Heaven was clear: to be sure of my stance as a son and as an inheritor of the Kingdom of God. I realized that I was not alone in this journey and that God was always with me, guiding me every step of the way. The seed that I will scatter is that of the awareness and revelation of

God's goodness and love. This is a revelation that cannot be found in religion but only in the loving arms of Jesus Christ.

# Chapter 16
# His Name is Revival

On the morning of February 11, 2023, while spending time with the Father in the Secret Place, I heard the voice of the Holy Spirit. He spoke, revealing that revival is breaking out in Indiana and Tennessee. The winds of revival will spread south to Florida and move from east to west—reaching from California to New York and even up to the highest points of Maine. This revival will be marked by a renewed passion for God and a deep desire to see His will fulfilled on Earth.

The Holy Spirit continued, saying that what the devil intended for evil will be turned for good for those who witness it. Those who have been lost or lukewarm in their faith will be drawn back to God and transformed by His love. This will be a season of spiritual renewal, with many turning to God as a result.

The Holy Spirit also spoke about the physical world, saying that there will be shifts and shakings in Earth's atmosphere. We will witness more meteor strikes and fireballs streaking across the sky than we did a decade ago.

The heavens will shake, the Earth will quake, and the hearts of men will be turned back to the awe and splendor of the Father.

Despite the world's hostility toward the love of God, the Holy Spirit has promised to transform people's hearts and draw them back to their first love. He said:

*This time will be marked by immense blessings and spiritual renewal, and we should be ready to receive all that God has in store for us.*

On February 14, just a few days after the promise had been made, I witnessed the beginning of its fulfillment. Reports began pouring in of revival breaking out across North America, starting at Asbury Seminary in Kentucky and spreading to other places like The Gate in Charlotte, North Carolina, Kings Way Church in Birmingham, Alabama, and many more.

As I read about these pockets of revival, I was filled with awe and wonder. The thought of people coming to know God and experiencing His love and power deeply moved me. I was so moved that I fell to my knees, weeping and repenting. I prayed that revival would break out in my own home and that my loved ones would experience the same joy and power that others were experiencing.

As I prayed, I had a vision of angels with sledgehammers smashing the hard ground. They were breaking up the soil to prepare it for the seeds of revival to be planted. I felt a sense of hope and excitement as I envisioned what God was doing in our nation and the hearts of His people.

Suddenly, I was taken into the Spirit and found myself on my face on the throne room floor. Before me stood a giant white marble bowl on a pedestal. Inside the bowl was fire, representing the prayers of those contending for revival and awakening across all generations, the prayers of both those in Heaven and on Earth. As I lay there, weeping and groaning, I could see through the throne room floor, and I was able to see the entire United States, even the whole Earth.

An angel stood before the Throne of God and scooped out the fire with something resembling a soup ladle combined with a slingshot. The angel flung each scoop of fire across the United States. I saw the fire marking specific cities and states—places like Oklahoma, Arkansas, North Dakota, Florida, Long Island, Louisiana, Los Angeles, Arizona, New Mexico, and many others. The fire landed and burned brightly in those places.

I then saw other angels holding scrolls the size of lances. These scrolls contained mandates for specific cities. I saw people in governmental offices weeping, falling on their faces, turning from wickedness, and repenting. It was one of the most beautiful sights—so many people turning back to God all at once.

I heard Heaven say: *"This is not just for the United States but for the whole Earth."*

Then I saw the Earth turn, and the hemisphere that was previously in darkness was now coming into light. I also saw fire being flung in other countries and continents, such as the Middle East, Asia, Europe, and Australia. As I watched, the image below panned back to the Earth, and suddenly, a tsunami of water washed across the entire North American continent from West to East. I heard in the spirit that this was the living water, a move of the Holy Spirit coming to wash and cleanse.

## The Refiners Fire

I heard the words, *"Do not let your heart be troubled or afraid, trust in God, trust also in Me."*

As I heard these words, I knew it was a call to engage with Heaven. In the flesh, I felt very weary, distraught, confused, and upset by the events that had unfolded that week in the natural realm. As I looked around, I saw Jesus.

However, as I gazed upon His beauty, I saw a waterfall in my spirit—pure and refreshing. He invited me to step under it, and as I did, I felt the water wash away my weariness, invigorating my soul. He called me His "beloved," and His gaze pierced my heart, breaking off the weights of the world from the week. The frequency of His pure love radiated into my heart and body. As these waves of glory washed over me, they shook off the chaff and revived me.

He said:

*Do not let your soul become downcast. The Father's promises are steadfast and true, but you live in a world bound by time. It gives birth to impatience, and impatience does not allow faith to have its perfect work in you or through you. Elevate your expectation, elevate your trust. Think of how long your forefathers waited for their promises. Did they waver in faith? Did they lose hope? Did they stop trusting in the Father? Oh, ye of little faith, be still and know God is with you. He will deliver you!*

*He will bless you and strengthen you to receive all that He has promised. If you are low on faith, ask for the faith of the Father. If you are low on hope, ask for hope to overflow from within you. Call upon the spirit of excellence to help you walk through sonship, and do not allow your expectations to grow dim. All trials are meant to help the children of God bear fruit and purify the saints.*

*Just remember that the challenges you have faced so far are like passing through a refiner's fire, but don't worry, the heat won't scorch you, and you won't be broken, crushed, or destroyed. You are moving towards a new level of greatness and authority.*

*Always walk with integrity and let wisdom guide you in all your actions. Be patient and know that what you desire is just around the corner. Don't let appearances in the physical realm weaken your faith, hope, and love.*

# Chapter 17
# King of My Heart

Early in the morning of April 16, 2023, I was deep in prayer when something miraculous happened. Jesus appeared before me and handed me three keys. These keys, He said, were meant to unlock my heart. He instructed me to use them to become a servant to my family through love, even in the face of frustration and hardship. I was initially taken aback, as my family had been under siege for what felt like an entire week. Nevertheless, I trusted in Jesus and took the keys.

He explained that each of the keys represented a different aspect of my life: the past, present, and future. He asked me to use them to unlock my heart, which had become calloused and closed off. As I inserted each key into the corresponding keyhole, I felt a sense of release and freedom. My heart had been unlocked, and a beautiful golden light flooded out of it.

At that moment, I knew that I needed Jesus more than ever before. He warned me not to let frustration and disappointment take root in my heart, as it could lead to bitterness and hard-heartedness. He cautioned me that even a single bitter root could spoil an entire garden, choking out any fruit that might grow from good soil.

Jesus urged me to forgive those whom I had held grudges against, as well as myself and my Father. He said that there might be hidden agreements and squatters in my being that needed to be evicted through repentance and a renewed cleansing. As I listened to Him speak, I felt a sense of relief and peace washing over me. I knew that with His help, I could love with His heart.

As He said this, the Holy Spirit drew me to Proverbs 23:26:

*My son, give your heart to Me, and let your eyes observe My ways. (Proverbs 23:26, TLV)*

I heard Jesus speaking and instructing me to be washed clean in His blood without any spot, wrinkle or defect. He also said that He would be coming back soon for a spotless bride. Jesus advised that His children keep their lamps filled with oil and their wicks trimmed so that our light can shine through these darkest hours.

## Reigniting the Hearts

In a subsequent encounter, I was taken up into a vision. I saw what looked like a treasure chest with thrones around it.

I was beckoned to come to this place. I could see the Father seated before me, and around Him were angels, men in white and others tending to him. I could see Jesus by His side. He said to me, *"My son, sit beside Me."* Jesus handed me a key and instructed me to open the chest before me. Inside, I saw a stone in the shape of a flame that glowed radiantly. It was orange like fire, yet tiny in size. As I held it in my hand, I began to weep. I could feel the Father's presence overcoming me in the spirit. I could see the spirits of my children and my wife also holding these stones in their little hands. I heard the Father say that this stone is representative of the fire of God. He told me to receive it into my heart.

I was told that I have been called in this season to expand into ministry to the men of God. The goal is to reawaken the fires of revival that have died and inspire a generation of men who hunger and thirst for intimacy with the Lord. They seek to break free from the shackles of the world and walk the path of righteousness.

As I stood there, I could see Wisdom approaching. She said, "You are a man of prudence." Then she handed me a cup to drink from. I was told that this was living water, the water of Wisdom's flow. As I drank this water, I was reminded of Proverbs 5, which teaches about the path of wisdom. It advises us to refrain from the way of immoral women and instead walk in the paths of integrity, sexual purity, holiness, righteousness and oneness in the covenant of marriage.

As this vision continued, I had a knowing in my spirit that the work the Lord wanted me to do in this season was to reach out to His sons and minister to them. Heaven said to be praying for those who are bound, at the same time that I was going through my own crushing, pressing and pruning. Father knew I felt vulnerable and just wanted to lay down and cry.

However, He said that this would give birth to a move of God so powerful that it would impact my future son-in-law, my sons, my grandchildren and future generations. I had a knowing that this would reignite, the desire for the deeper things of God in the lives of the men. His sons had been lost working and laboring out in the fields, He wanted them to come home. They had lost sight of the beauty, the holiness, and the splendor of being in covenant with Father. His desire was for all the men to be walking in lockstep with Him.

I became aware of the places where I had grown lukewarm or complacent, and in my heart burned a desire to turn from that path and seek the Father. I cried out to be held, and to be loved, that my wounds would be healed, that I would be restored, and then I would mirror Jesus in all things. As I wept, He came and comforted me as only our Heavenly Father can do.

On another occasion, the Holy Spirit said:

*This is the way, My child; walk in it; walk in love. Let your light shine before men, and let your deeds glorify the Father in Heaven. His light provides a multitude of things, but it's most powerful attribute is the unfailing love of the Father.*

The instinctive overflow of every molecule in the human body resonates with the frequency of this love. As the living water flows through you, others will feel the presence of Glory all around. Do not hold back from the full expression of the Father's undying devotion for all His children; to live is Christ to die is gain. The verse John 16:22 dropped into my spirit:

*So also, you have sorrow now; but I will see you again, and your heart will rejoice, and no one will take your joy away from you! (John 16:22, AMP)*

Holy Spirit continued,

*This is a season of rejoicing in merriment and much celebration upon the Earth, but in the heavenly places, there's more rejoicing in celebration than one could imagine. Times and seasons of the Earth's calendar conflict with the times and seasons of Heaven's calendar but it is a time of celebration of new newness of life. This is the time of celebration of revival, it is the time of celebration of the King returning. Do not be confused or deluded by the hypocrisy of man.*

*Much lawlessness still runs rampant upon the Earth. Many diabolical plans are still concocted by the enemy's camp. They still tirelessly try to execute them; however, their plans are plans of failure. They have already been judged, and the Father's righteous hand is against all who exalt themselves above His name.*

*Do not pay attention to the media. Do not pay mind to the news or that which will seek to confuse. Do not pay mind to reports of disease, or reports of famine. Seek first the Kingdom of God.*

*Set your mind on the throne of Heaven and lean not on your own understanding. Know that the Lord will lead and guide those who trust in Him. They shall be untouched throughout all the darkness of the land, for He is your light; He will light the way of your path.*

*It's time to war against all the spirits that have been trying to attack you. The all-out offensive assault is being watched, even as we speak, by the righteous armies of Heaven. They are going to war on your behalf.*

*New angels are being sent to partner with your angels and the angels of all those who serve the*

*Kingdom of God. There will be a reckoning in this season. Lawlessness will be cast down, and righteous pillars for the Throne of God will be set up across the land.*

## Juggling Life

In another encounter, I found myself face to face with the Father. He spoke words of love to me, and their warmth filled my heart with comfort and peace. Then, with a surprising yet graceful motion, He began to juggle five objects resembling delicate, glowing spheres. I stood in awe, captivated by His effortless precision as He tossed them up and down with what seemed like a single hand.

At one point, He tossed the spheres toward me, inviting me to continue juggling. But as I tried to catch them, each one slipped through my fingers and shattered on the ground like fragile eggs. Gently, He explained that I was carrying too much, trying to manage more than I could handle.

With a kind smile, He lifted me onto His shoulders and began to walk with me. As we strolled together, He revealed glimpses of Heaven and spoke wisdom into my life, offering clarity and guidance for my career. His presence, tender yet powerful, filled me with renewed hope and assurance that I was not meant to carry the weight of life alone.

As we continued walking, His voice resonated with love and wisdom, guiding me toward a clearer vision of my future. He spoke of the ways I could collaborate with the angels to achieve success, growth, and expansion in every area of my life. Each word ignited a deep sense of purpose and direction that I hadn't fully realized before.

He showed me the beauty in my family life and recreational activities—areas I sometimes took for granted—and revealed that they were about to flourish in ways I couldn't yet imagine. My heart overflowed with gratitude for the blessings I had already received and excitement for the transformation to come.

Then, my gaze was drawn to Heaven Down™ Business. I saw it blossoming into something extraordinary, filled with vitality and growth. It was humbling and exhilarating to know that my role in this business was meaningful and that Father recognized and appreciated my efforts.

He shifted my focus to my ministry, showing me how it was budding with promise. He assured me it would soon blossom into something far-reaching and impactful. The vision filled me with purpose and a deep sense of fulfillment, knowing that my calling was aligned with His plans.

Finally, Father turned His attention to my graphic design business. To my surprise, He revealed that it was about to experience remarkable growth. The thought of expansion filled me with joy, but He also warned that I would need to prepare for this by bringing on an assistant. The vision of my business thriving and my hard work paying off was exhilarating, and I felt a renewed determination to steward these opportunities with care and diligence.

Heaven instructed me to build the necessary infrastructure to support the growth of my businesses. It was a reminder that with success comes responsibility, and I was ready to take on the challenge.

Father's words were like a salve to my soul, addressing the challenges we faced in adjusting to life in the south. He assured me that even in this season of difficulty, there was divine purpose. He cautioned me against allowing offense to take root and harden my heart. Instead, He called me to trust that this challenging road was part of a larger plan, one that would refine and strengthen me. He reminded me that we were serving Him, not people, in this place.

His encouragement was clear and direct:

*You are not doing anything wrong related to your growth path, do not let anyone derail you. Stop taking instruction from others and seek it from Me!*

Those words pierced through my doubts and brought a clarity that I hadn't realized I needed.

As the engagement ended, a profound understanding settled in my spirit. I meditated on the truth of John 12:22-26, where Jesus speaks of the kernel of wheat falling to the ground and dying to produce many seeds. I realized that I was in the midst of a spiritual process of death—a process that involved crushing, pressing, and allowing my flesh to be brought into submission.

This process, though painful, was not without purpose. It was part of an eternal transformation that would continue until the day I transitioned to Glory. I began to see the beauty of this refining season. Like fruit growing season after season, my life would yield an ongoing harvest, provided I remained connected to the vine and embraced the pruning.

Father impressed upon me the importance of leaning into the crushing and the pressing. These moments of discomfort and surrender were not punishments but gifts, designed to produce growth and maturity. In the midst of it all, He assured me that fruit would come, that it would be abundant and beautiful, and that it would bring glory to His name.

I left this encounter with renewed hope and a deeper understanding of the eternal perspective I needed to carry. Every challenge, every hardship, and every moment of pressing was not just for my benefit but for the greater purpose of bearing fruit that would last. This revelation gave me the strength to face the road ahead with faith, courage, and a heart set on Him.

# Chapter 18

# He Speaks Peace to the Storms

In His infinite goodness, the Father never abandons us, even in the most challenging seasons of life. His steadfast presence and unwavering love remain constant, regardless of how difficult our circumstances may seem. As I continued to grow in my understanding of sonship and the boundless love of the Father, I found myself stretched in ways I had never imagined. This season of growth, though necessary, was anything but comfortable.

It is often said that moving is one of the most stressful experiences a person can endure, and I was living proof of that reality. However, the challenge wasn't merely about packing boxes or navigating a new location; it was the emotional toll it took on me and my family. As a husband and father, I felt the weight of not only my own burdens but also those of my wife and children.

My natural inclination as a husband and father was to be a fixer. I wanted to shield my family from pain, take ownership of their struggles, and provide solutions for every issue we faced. It seemed noble, even necessary, to assume this role. Yet, I quickly discovered the flaw in my thinking: I am not God, and it was never my responsibility to carry such a heavy load.

This realization was a hard lesson to learn. It challenged everything in me that wanted to protect and provide for those I loved. But in the midst of my striving, the Father spoke to my heart with gentle clarity: *"For my yoke is easy, and my burden is light"*(Matthew 11:30).

One morning, I was feeling overwhelmed by my emotions and the burden of what my wife and children were going through in the transition season. As always, I did what I knew to do, which was seek Heaven's suggestions on how to navigate.

As I peered into the spirit, I could see myself and my family on a dinghy being. This small vessel was being tossed about as it sailed upon choppy waters. The ferocious intensity of the waves around grew in magnitude, and suddenly, a crackle of lighting split the dark, stormy skies. Rain started pouring down in buckets as the waves tossed the vessel about.

I could see myself on the boat trying to find sure footing. There with us was Jesus, looking marvelously at peace and completely undisturbed by the storm around. As I watched this scene play out, I heard the Father tell me, *"Do not be moved or dismayed by the storms of life."*

He said:

*No matter the intensity My son, be at peace, be still. Your heart has been affected by each instance of hardship, confusion, and even doubt as of late. These are all storms, oppositional attacks of the enemy, made to shift your focus and throw you off course. They are tricks meant to divert you from what you are called to do. Focus your heart and your ear on all Heaven has for you.*

*Listen closely to My voice, let My heartbeat guide your decisions, and allow My presence to soothe your weary soul. Ships get shipwrecked under the wake of waves, but your faith will not be shipwrecked as you are tried and tested. Allow the Glory to settle your spirit. Lean on Me when you are weak, and I will become your strength. Don't get lost in the frailties of life and the responsibilities of what you feel you have to do. All you have to do is hold your peace; I will fight for you.*

# Walking the Narrow Path

As our dialogue continued, Father began to inform me of things to come in our new assignment and our new home state of Florida.

He said:

*The road before you is long, narrow and winding, but the destination is beautiful; it is glory-filled and radiating the incandescent resonant frequencies of the heavenly realm. This path is paved with gold and mountains of silver; let knowledge, wisdom, and understanding guide you.*

*You have stepped onto the page of a new chapter with your wife, together with this ministry (The Safehouse Church), with new friends, divine connections, and destinations not yet seen. Trust My promptings, obey My voice, listen to My instructions, and watch for the signs. You asked for more signs, and in kindness I will show you many. Those around you see what I see, and the time is now for you to behold your own heart and the way in which I crafted you. I see your delicacy in the way you speak and act. I know your heart's intent and true desire, and I have tested it to ensure it is not faulty in its desire to serve Me wholeheartedly. Battles and storms will come, but I will establish you on a rock foundation and shelter you during the storms. Prepare to be blissfully supported as what I am bringing into the natural realm manifests itself before your eyes. You will see, My child; you will feel My presence; you will see in the spirit and the natural and understand what I have called you to do. Fret not, be still, and know that the time is at hand for advancement into the new season; the new door of destiny is opening. Stay the course!*

*Sometimes, you must leave where you are comfortable and step onto the mission field. You will be connected in the ways I want you to be. If you ask Me, I will order your steps to make things easy. The heart can be deceiving, but My will for you is secured in My love for you.*

Father could sense my mind was wandering into concern for my family and He put His hand on my shoulder reassuringly and said, "Your wife and children will be happiest and thriving in the South. I want you to have prophetic mothering and fathering; It is time to step into the fullness of your destiny and calling." As He spoke, I saw visions of the drug-addicted, hopeless, and broken coming for prayer and receiving salvation.

The Father said, *"There will be many invited to The Safehouse, and many invited to its conferences; it will be a house of transformation and a habitation of My Glory."*

As He spoke, I could see into the timeline of our new assignment. I saw the house being built not just as a physical structure but as *His* house. He showed me many ministers and people coming together to help build this house, each contributing their unique gifts and talents. In that moment, I understood that if I trusted His plan, everything would unfold according to His will, and all would be well.

Then, the following scripture from Deuteronomy dropped into my spirit, and as I read it, I could feel His presence washing over me, filling me with peace and assurance. Each word seemed to settle deeply into my heart, reaffirming the blessings He was preparing for us.

> *¹ Now if you listen obediently to the voice of ADONAI your God, taking care to do all His mitzvot that I am commanding you today, ADONAI your God will set you on high—above all the nations of the Earth.*

> *² Then all these blessings will come upon you and overtake you, if you listen to the voice of ADONAI your God:*

> *³ Blessed will you be in the city, and blessed will you be in the field.*

> *⁴ Blessed will be the fruit of your womb, the produce of your soil, and the offspring of your livestock—the increase of your herds and the young of your flock.*

⁵ *Blessed will be your basket and your kneading bowl.*

⁶ *Blessed will you be when you come in, and blessed will you be when you go out.*

⁷ *ADONAI will cause your enemies who rise up against you to be struck down before you. They will come out against you one way and flee before you seven ways.*

⁸ *ADONAI will command the blessing on you in your barns and in every undertaking of your hand, and He will bless you in the land ADONAI your God is giving you.*

⁹ *ADONAI will establish you as a holy people for Himself, just as He swore to you—if you keep the mitzvot of ADONAI your God and walk in His ways.*

¹⁰ *Then all the peoples of the Earth will see that you are called by the name of ADONAI, and they will stand in awe of you.*

¹¹ *ADONAI will make you overflow in prosperity—in the fruit of your womb, the offspring of your livestock and the produce of your soil—on the land ADONAI swore to your fathers to give you.*

¹² *ADONAI will open for you His good storehouse— the heavens—to give rain for your land in its season*

*and to bless all the work of your hand. You will lend to many nations, but you will not borrow.*

*[13] ADONAI will make you the head and not the tail, and you will be only above and not below—if you listen to the mitzvot of ADONAI your God that I am commanding you today, careful to do them,*

*[14] and do not turn aside from any of the words I am commanding you today, to the right or the left, to go after other gods in order to serve them (Deuteronomy 28:1-14, TLV).*

As this engagement came to a close, my perceptions had been shifted by the Father's love. No longer did I dread change and uncertainty. I was optimistically looking for His goodness in every step and decision, and as I expected His goodness, the Goodness of God became my harvest.

Stay in faith and expectation of the Father to move the mountains in your life, and the goodness of God will overtake you, too, in every season and every situation. This level of relationship with Heaven is for all to experience. We must only ask Him, and it shall given to us. Seek His Kingdom, and we shall find it and knock so that the door to His heart will be opened to us.[10]

---

# Epilogue

Friends, we have a choice to make. As His children, Father will always bless us, even if we miss His timing. However, deep within, we will always know when we've missed His best for us.

Humanity has been on Earth for around 6,000 years, and throughout that time, we've often allowed the enemy to divert us from the mark. As sons and daughters of the Kingdom, we are called to fulfill specific assignments, and we should honor that commitment. Our mission is to demonstrate the true Kingdom of God without hesitation or compromise. Since the fall of Eden, both people and creation have been longing for this revelation.

As tough as it has been for Jeremy and his family to move and endure all the inner reconstruction, they are committed to God's highest standard. Though the process has been challenging, and there's still more ahead, the flow of blessing from Heaven is making the struggles seem small in comparison to the results already beginning to unfold.

Be encouraged—if we can do this, so can you! Engage the experiences shared as if they were your own. Enlarge your field of influence and get ready for Heaven to reveal rare insights that will bless you and equip you to pass those blessings on to others. Isn't that what sonship is truly about?

Take a moment to pause—what do you hear? Do you hear the cry? If so, simply ask, "Lord, what can I do?" And Heaven will respond.

*– Dr. Robert Rodich*

# Description

Discover the Heart of the Father Through Heavenly Encounters

In *The Heart of the Father*, Jeremy Friedman shares his deeply personal journey of stepping into Heaven to commune with the Father, Jesus, the Holy Spirit, and other heavenly beings. Through this practice, Jeremy found comfort, guidance, and renewed faith while navigating some of life's most difficult challenges.

This reflective and encouraging book explores the profound intimacy that comes from engaging the heavenlies with faith. Jeremy reveals insights into the Father's character, how He communicates, and the transformative power of encountering Him in spirit.

Designed as both testimony and guide, this book offers a blueprint for believers seeking to deepen their relationship with God. Through relatable trials and moments of doubt, Jeremy shows how God's love and wisdom are always available to those who seek Him.

For those ready to explore a deeper relationship with the Father, *The Heart of the Father* offers a glimpse of Heaven's love and encouragement, showing how engaging the Father in spirit can transform life's journey.

# About the Author

Jeremy Friedman is a prophetic teacher, evangelist, intercessor, and entrepreneur with a unique apostolic grace. His life testimony is a powerful example of God's saving power, and through his journey to faith, he has helped many others understand the heart of the Father. Jeremy's prophetic gifting enables him to perceive the world in ways that often go unnoticed, allowing him to offer deeper insights into spiritual matters.

Daily, he seeks the Lord with his whole heart, longing to receive revelation from Heaven to help build God's Kingdom on Earth. As a Jewish believer in Yeshua, Jeremy has a passion to serve as a bridge between all nations, helping people understand that they are grafted into the rich Jewish heritage of the Bible through our Messiah.

Currently, Jeremy is the founder of *Lighthouse Family Ministries*, the host of the *Frequency of Heaven* podcast, head coach for *Heaven Down™ Business*, and a key member of the *LifeSpring International Ministries* team. He is deeply committed to deliverance ministry, helping others find the same freedom he has experienced. As a devoted husband and father of five beautiful children, Jeremy is committed to raising his family in faith, hoping they will walk in their callings and teach future generations to rise and build the Kingdom of Heaven.

Published by:

Scroll
PUBLISHERS

A division of LifeSpring Publishing
www.scrollpublishers.com

Has God spoken to you about writing a book?
Let us help you!

www.ingramcontent.com/pod-product-compliance
Lightning Source LLC
Chambersburg PA
CBHW021226090426
42740CB00006B/399